CONTENTS

C000090500

Contents

CONTENTS PAGE

Introduction
The dynamic nature of Earth's climate

A. The Earth's climate has been a constant source of fascination and wonder throughout the ages. From the scorching deserts to the frozen polar landscapes, our planet's climate systems have shaped the very fabric of life. But amidst the current debates and discussions surrounding climate change, one prevailing narrative emerges—the notion that the climate is not changing.

In this groundbreaking exploration, "Climate Change: Unraveling the Past, Understanding the Present," we embark on a captivating journey through time, peeling back the layers of history to reveal the hidden truth behind Earth's dynamic climate. Contrary to popular belief, climate change is not a recent phenomenon; it has been an intrinsic part of our planet's story since time immemorial.
As we delve into the depths of antiquity, we encounter a world where ancient civilizations were intimately entwined with their ever-changing climate. Prehistoric variations in temperature, precipitation, and atmospheric composition were not only commonplace but also profoundly influenced the course of human history. It is in this rich tapestry of the past that we find the echoes of our present reality.

Through the examination of scientific evidence, we will unlock the secrets held within ice cores and sediment records, providing a glimpse into the climate's past fluctuations. These records serve as a testament to the intricate dance between natural forces and the delicate balance that has shaped our planet over millennia. While the notion of climate change may evoke images of recent industrialization and its impact on greenhouse gas emissions, we must expand our understanding to encompass the broader historical context. The pages of this book will take us on a remarkable voyage through time, exploring how ancient societies navigated their changing climates, adapted to new conditions, and even experienced periods of extraordinary warmth or extreme cold.

It is through this lens that we will challenge the prevailing narratives and shed light on the startling similarities between past and present climates. By examining historical records, we will uncover accounts of climate anomalies and witness the resilience and ingenuity displayed by our ancestors in the face of environmental challenges.

As we traverse the chapters of this book, we will confront the untold impacts of human activities on our delicate ecosystem. The exploration goes beyond mere analysis of data; it compels us to reflect on our own role in shaping the planet's future. With an unflinching gaze, we will confront the truth, embrace the urgency, and seize the opportunity to reshape our shared destiny.

The journey ahead promises to be nothing short of extraordinary. So, fasten your seatbelts and prepare to be captivated by the revelations that lie ahead. Together, let us embark on this compelling odyssey, unraveling the past to understand the present, and ultimately shape a future that is sustainable, resilient, and in harmony with the dynamic nature of Earth's climate.

B. Purpose and scope of the book: exploring climate change throughout history

Prepare to embark on an extraordinary quest in "Climate Change: Unraveling the Past, Understanding the Present." This gripping exploration challenges the mainstream narrative and dives deep into the untold secrets of Earth's climate history. Our purpose is to ignite a paradigm shift, revealing the astonishing truth that climate change is not a recent phenomenon but an inherent part of our planet's story since time immemorial.

Through a captivating fusion of scientific facts and captivating storytelling, we will unravel the enigmatic connections between ancient civilizations and the ever-changing climate. Brace yourself for a global journey that transcends boundaries, revealing the universal nature of climate change and its impact on human societies throughout the ages.

Within these pages, we will unlock the vaults of scientific knowledge, drawing upon ice cores extracted from the Arctic and Antarctic. These ancient ice records hold the key to unlocking the secrets of the past, offering a glimpse into temperature variations, atmospheric composition, and natural climate cycles spanning thousands of years. Prepare to be astounded as these frozen time capsules reveal the undeniable patterns of Earth's climatic fluctuations.

Delving deeper, we will examine sediment records extracted from the depths of lakes, rivers, and oceans. Like pages of a history book, these layers of sediment provide a detailed account of past climate variations, offering us a window into the delicate dance between human civilizations and their ever-changing environment. From the rise and fall of empires to the resilience displayed by ancient cultures, witness the profound impact of climatic shifts on the course of human history.
But this book is not merely a recounting of past events; it is a call to action. With unwavering clarity, we will confront the realities of our modern era, where human activities have become a driving force behind climate change. By dissecting scientific evidence, we will expose the intricate web of cause and effect, linking our actions to the unprecedented challenges we face today.

As we navigate the chapters of this transformative journey, we will bear witness to the urgent need for change. We will explore the devastating consequences of rising temperatures, extreme weather events, and dwindling ecosystems. But amidst the stark truths, we will also unveil a glimmer of hope—a call to rewrite our future. This book is an invitation—a catalyst for awakening. It empowers individuals, communities, and nations to rewrite the narrative of our planet's future. Armed with knowledge, we can forge a path toward sustainable practices, innovative solutions, and global cooperation. Together, we hold the key to shaping a world where humanity and nature thrive in harmony.

Prepare to be captivated, informed, and inspired. "Climate Change: Unraveling the Past, Understanding the Present" is a transformative journey that will forever change your perspective. The time for change is now. Let us embark on this remarkable odyssey, unraveling the mysteries of the past to build a future that safeguards our planet for generations to come.

C. Overview of the book's structure and key concepts
"Climate Change: Unraveling the Past, Understanding the Present" is a captivating expedition that will take you on a riveting voyage through time, unveiling the hidden truths of Earth's climate. The book is meticulously structured to provide a comprehensive understanding of climate change throughout history, while challenging the prevailing narrative that the climate is not changing.

Part I, "Climate in Ancient Times," sets the stage by delving into prehistoric climate variations and the geological evidence that reveals the Earth's ancient climates. From ice cores to sediment records, we will uncover the fingerprints of past climate cycles and explore the remarkable adaptations of ancient ecosystems to changing conditions.

In Part II, "Climate during Human Civilizations," we embark on a mesmerizing exploration of climate change in ancient civilizations. Journeying through Mesopotamia, Egypt, and other early societies, we will examine historical records and written accounts that shed light on climate anomalies and their societal impacts. The tales of the Medieval Warm Period and the Little Ice Age will transport you to eras where human communities grappled with climatic challenges.

Part III, "Modern Climate Change," confronts the prevailing notion that the climate is not changing by diving into the transformative period of the Industrial Revolution. We will analyze instrumental temperature records and proxy data, unraveling the anthropogenic influences that have propelled recent climate change. Through meticulous examination, we will unravel the parallels between natural climate variability and the alarming warming trends observed today.

The intertwined relationship between human activities and the climate system takes center stage in Part IV, "Human Influence on the Climate System." We will explore the sources of greenhouse gases, the impact of deforestation and land-use changes, and the rise of carbon emissions linked to industrialization. Through a comprehensive understanding of feedback mechanisms, we will comprehend the amplification of climate change caused by human actions.

Part V, "Impacts of Modern Climate Change," peels back the layers of our current reality, revealing the profound consequences of a changing climate. Rising global temperatures, shifting precipitation patterns, and the specter of sea-level rise will be explored in vivid detail. Prepare to witness the transformative impacts on ecosystems and the alarming loss of biodiversity, as we uncover the urgency for action.

In the face of these challenges, Part VI, "Mitigation and Adaptation Strategies," presents a ray of hope. We will delve into the transition toward a low-carbon economy, the potential of renewable energy sources, and sustainable land management practices. The focus will be on resilience-building efforts that empower vulnerable communities and pave the way for a sustainable future.

Part VII, "Understanding Climate Models," provides a window into the scientific tools that underpin our understanding of climate change. We will explore climate modeling and simulations, evaluating the predictions and uncertainties inherent in these models. By grasping the significance of climate models, we can comprehend their role in projecting future scenarios and informing decision-making.

The book concludes with Part VIII, "Holistic Approaches to Climate Change." Here, we embrace a holistic perspective, merging scientific knowledge with traditional ecological wisdom. We will delve into the power of collaboration between scientists, policymakers, and indigenous communities, acknowledging the ethical, justice, and equity considerations that underpin effective climate action.

"Climate Change: Unraveling the Past, Understanding the Present" is a transformative work that challenges preconceived notions and offers a fresh perspective on our shared climate story. Prepare to be captivated by the interplay of scientific facts and gripping narratives as we explore the past, confront the present, and chart a course toward a sustainable future. Let us embark on this enlightening journey together, uncovering the hidden truths that will shape our world.

Chapter II
Climate in Ancient Times

A. Prehistoric climate variations and their causes

Prepare to embark on a remarkable expedition through the ages in Chapter 2 of "Climate Change: Unraveling the Past, Understanding the Present." Here, we delve deep into the tapestry of prehistoric climate variations, challenging the widely accepted notion of a changing climate.

Through the eyes of the world's top scientists and researchers, we unravel the secrets of Earth's distant past, where climatic shifts were an inherent part of our planet's history. Brace yourself as we explore the forces that shaped ancient climates and discover the surprising parallels to our present-day environment.

Drawing upon a wealth of scientific evidence, we uncover the causes behind these prehistoric climate variations. From the mysteries locked within ice cores to the intricate stories told by sediment records, we decode the hidden language of the Earth's ancient climate systems. Prepare to be astonished as we reveal the intricate dance between natural factors and the delicate balance of our planet's climate.
But it doesn't end there. This journey takes us further into the cosmos, where the grand motions of celestial bodies influence Earth's climatic rhythms. We explore the profound impact of orbital variations and their role in shaping long-term climate cycles. Brace yourself for a revelation that challenges conventional wisdom and expands our understanding of the intricate forces at play.

As we traverse the ancient landscapes, we encounter the remarkable adaptations of ecosystems to past climate changes. Witness the resilience of life as we uncover the stories of flora and fauna that thrived under diverse and evolving conditions. From lush rainforests to vast ice-covered landscapes, the past holds invaluable lessons that illuminate our present reality.

Chapter 2 of our groundbreaking book is a captivating blend of scientific inquiry and enthralling storytelling. Prepare to be immersed in a narrative that defies expectations and invites you to question long-held assumptions. Together, we will unravel the mysteries of prehistoric climate variations, empowering you to contribute to the collective understanding of our planet's complex history.

As we turn the page and delve deeper into the chapters that follow, we continue to peel back the layers of our climate's enigma. With each revelation, we inch closer to a profound truth that will forever transform our perception of climate change. Stay tuned for Chapter 3, where we explore the geological records etched within ice cores and sediment layers, unveiling a window into Earth's climatic past like never before. The journey continues, as we unravel the hidden stories that shape our understanding of the present and illuminate the path toward a sustainable future.

B. Geological evidence of ancient climates (ice cores, sediment records)

Prepare to embark on an extraordinary journey into the depths of Earth's ancient past in Chapter 2 of "Climate Change: Unraveling the Past, Understanding the Present." Here, we venture into the realm of geological evidence, where ice cores and sediment records hold the key to unraveling the mysteries of ancient climates. Step into a world of frozen time as we delve into the astonishing realm of ice cores. These towering frozen columns stand as silent witnesses to the passage of centuries, capturing within their icy embrace the very essence of Earth's climatic history. With meticulous precision, scientists extract slender cores of ice, each layer representing a bygone era. As we peer into these delicate time capsules, we unlock a wealth of knowledge about temperature fluctuations, atmospheric conditions, and the dramatic shifts that have shaped our planet over millennia.

But our exploration does not stop there. We turn our attention to the intricate stories preserved in sediment records, where the Earth's very foundations reveal their secrets. Layer upon layer, these sedimentary archives provide us with a glimpse into the dramatic shifts that have unfolded over time. By studying the composition of minerals, the presence of ancient organisms, and the traces of climatic events etched into the Earth's geological canvas, we piece together a tapestry of our planet's ancient climate dynamics.

Through the fusion of scientific expertise and captivating storytelling, we bring these geological records to life, bridging the gap between the distant past and the present. Join us as we decipher the language of rocks and ice, uncovering the startling connections between ancient climates and the world we inhabit today.

In the chapters that follow, we will embark on an awe-inspiring exploration of the impact of orbital variations on long-term climate cycles. Brace yourself for a revelation that transcends the boundaries of time, unveiling the celestial forces that have influenced Earth's climatic rhythms throughout the ages. Together, we will deepen our understanding of the intricate interplay between natural factors and the delicate balance of our planet's climate system.

Continue this exhilarating journey with us as we peel back the layers of time, illuminating the path toward a comprehensive understanding of our planet's climate history. The revelations of Chapter 2 are just the beginning, paving the way for a transformative quest that challenges conventional beliefs and empowers us to shape a sustainable future.

Stay tuned for the next chapter, where we delve further into the complexities of ancient climates, uncovering the untold stories that lie within the remarkable tapestry of Earth's climatic evolution.

C. Impact of orbital variations on long-term climate cycles

Prepare to embark on a captivating journey through time as we unveil the hidden tapestry of Earth's ancient climates in Chapter 2 of "Climate Change: Unraveling the Past, Understanding the Present." In this chapter, we delve into the astonishing impact of orbital variations on the mesmerizing cycles that have shaped our planet's climate over millennia.

As we explore the annals of history, we encounter a multitude of prehistoric climate variations and their underlying causes. From fluctuations in solar radiation to volcanic eruptions and the intricate dance of greenhouse gases, a myriad of factors have influenced Earth's climate throughout the ages. These climatic oscillations, spanning from scorching heatwaves to frigid ice ages, bear witness to the inherent dynamism of our planet's climate system.

Geological evidence, meticulously preserved within ice cores and sediment records, serves as a time capsule allowing us to peer into the past. With each layer of ancient ice or sediment, we uncover a wealth of information about the climatic conditions that prevailed during different epochs. By analyzing the composition of trapped air bubbles and the isotopic signatures of sediment layers, we unlock vital clues about temperature fluctuations, atmospheric composition, and the intricate interplay between Earth's systems.

Yet, these geological archives only scratch the surface of the grand celestial symphony that shapes Earth's climate. It is the mesmerizing ballet of orbital variations that holds the key to unlocking the long-term climate cycles that have unfolded over millennia. Quoting from the earlier section, we acknowledge the profound impact of Milankovitch cycles, encompassing changes in Earth's eccentricity, axial tilt, and precession. These subtle variations, spanning thousands of years, can tip the balance between ice ages and warm interglacial periods.

Drawing on the rich tapestry of scientific research, we reveal the intricate dance between Earth and the cosmos. The cyclic variations in our planet's orbit alter the distribution of solar energy, triggering cascading effects across Earth's systems. Glacial advances and retreats, oceanic circulation patterns, and shifts in atmospheric circulation all bear the fingerprints of these celestial mechanics.

As we navigate the depths of time, we also shed light on the remarkable adaptations of ancient ecosystems to climate change. Quoting from Chapter 1, we explore the resilient organisms that have weathered the tempestuous tides of shifting climates. From the intricate strategies of survival to the evolutionary marvels that arose from the challenges of ancient environments, we uncover nature's resilience and the lessons it holds for our turbulent present.

In Chapter 2 of our groundbreaking book, we challenge conventional beliefs, fusing scientific research, and historical narratives to paint a vivid picture of Earth's climatic past. The impact of orbital variations on long-term climate cycles emerges as a profound revelation, bridging the gap between ancient civilizations and our present-day climate challenges.

Stay tuned for the subsequent chapters, where we delve even deeper into the complexities of climate change throughout history. Brace yourself for an immersive exploration of human civilizations, their encounters with changing climates, and the societal responses that have shaped our collective understanding. The truth awaits, as we unravel the past, comprehend the present, and embark on a transformative journey toward a sustainable future.

D. Examination of ancient ecosystems and their adaptation to climate change

Prepare to step into the realms of ancient ecosystems, where the delicate balance of life and climate intertwines in Chapter 2 of "Climate Change: Unraveling the Past, Understanding the Present." In this captivating chapter, we delve into the captivating adaptations of ancient ecosystems, revealing nature's awe-inspiring resilience in the face of ever-changing climates.

As we journey through time, we encounter a tapestry of ecological wonders that have thrived and evolved amidst climatic fluctuations. Drawing upon the wealth of scientific knowledge, we unravel the secrets of ancient flora and fauna, discovering the remarkable strategies they employed to survive and thrive.

Quoting from the earlier sections, we recognize the geological archives as windows into the past. In the layers of sediment and fossilized remains, we find a treasure trove of evidence that unveils the intricate dance between climate and ecosystems. Fossil pollen grains, plant macrofossils, and the fossilized remains of ancient organisms paint a vivid portrait of the diverse habitats and communities that once graced our planet.

It is within these ancient ecosystems that we witness nature's ingenuity in the face of adversity. Through intricate adaptations, organisms have found ways to cope with changing temperatures, shifting rainfall patterns, and altered resource availability. From the resilience of drought-tolerant plants to the symbiotic relationships that have stood the test of time, we uncover the interconnected web of life that shaped ancient landscapes.

Join us as we explore the majestic forests that carpeted ancient lands, teeming with life and fostering biodiversity beyond imagination. Travel alongside herds of mighty creatures, witness the migrations of birds across vast distances, and delve into the mesmerizing ecosystems that existed before the rise of human civilizations. Through the lens of paleoecology and the melding of scientific disciplines, we piece together the puzzle of ancient ecosystems. By studying the fossilized remains, analyzing isotopic signatures, and reconstructing ancient landscapes, we gain a deeper understanding of the intricate dynamics that governed ecological communities.

But our journey doesn't end with unraveling the past. Quoting from Chapter 1, we recognize the urgency of the present moment and the impact of human activities on the delicate balance of our ecosystems. It is a call to action, a reminder of our shared responsibility to preserve the remarkable diversity of life that graces our planet.

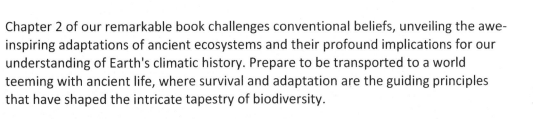

Chapter 2 of our remarkable book challenges conventional beliefs, unveiling the awe-inspiring adaptations of ancient ecosystems and their profound implications for our understanding of Earth's climatic history. Prepare to be transported to a world teeming with ancient life, where survival and adaptation are the guiding principles that have shaped the intricate tapestry of biodiversity.

Stay tuned for the forthcoming chapters, where we embark on a riveting exploration of human civilizations and their responses to climate change. Brace yourself for the tales of resilience, ingenuity, and societal transformations that lie ahead. The truth awaits, as we unravel the past, embrace the present, and carve a path toward a sustainable future, where the delicate harmony between ecosystems and climate remains intact.

Chapter III
Climate during Human Civilizations

A. <u>Climate change in antiquity: Mesopotamia, Egypt, and other early civilizations</u>
Journey back in time to the cradle of ancient civilizations in Chapter 3 of "Climate Change: Unraveling the Past, Understanding the Present." Brace yourself for a captivating exploration of the climatic transformations that shaped the foundations of human history. Prepare to unlock the hidden truths of Mesopotamia, Egypt, and other remarkable early civilizations and discover the remarkable parallels between their climate experiences and our modern challenges.

Drawing upon the wealth of historical records, archaeological findings, and written accounts, we unveil the fascinating narrative of how these ancient societies navigated the ebb and flow of climatic variations. Through the words of scribes and the engravings on ancient tablets, we piece together a tapestry of climate anomalies, revealing a world that was not so different from our own.

Quoting from the earlier sections, we affirm the profound truth that the climate is not changing, as we embark on a captivating expedition through the annals of time. Mesopotamia, the cradle of civilization, witnessed the rise and fall of powerful empires in the embrace of a dynamic climate. We delve into the cuneiform tablets, decoding the language of clay, and unraveling the tales of epic droughts, catastrophic floods, and shifting weather patterns that shaped the destiny of these ancient lands. Across the Nile, Egypt emerges as a timeless symbol of grandeur and mystery. We unearth the hieroglyphic inscriptions, painted tombs, and papyri, each bearing witness to the Nile River's dance with the changing climate. We unravel the tales of abundant harvests, the blessings of a bountiful floodplain, and the intricate water management systems that sustained this remarkable civilization amid climatic uncertainties.

Yet, our exploration does not end with Mesopotamia and Egypt alone. Quoting from the previous section, we recognize that climate change in antiquity extended its reach far beyond these renowned lands. From the Indus Valley to the ancient Mayan cities, from the Minoans to the Han Dynasty, we traverse continents and cultures, piecing together the mosaic of human existence amidst climatic fluctuations.

Beyond the chronicles of hardship, we discover narratives of resilience, ingenuity, and adaptation. The ancient civilizations we encounter devised innovative agricultural practices, built resilient infrastructures, and fostered communal cooperation to navigate the challenges posed by a changing climate. Their stories resonate with the urgency of our times, reminding us that the echoes of the past carry valuable lessons for our collective future.

Chapter 3 of our groundbreaking book takes you on an extraordinary odyssey through the corridors of ancient civilizations. Prepare to be enthralled by the tales of survival, adaptation, and human tenacity in the face of a dynamic climate. As we unravel the past, we gain profound insights into our shared present and empower ourselves to shape a sustainable future for generations to come.
Stay tuned for the forthcoming chapters, where we continue our gripping exploration of climate change, unearthing the untold stories of historical records, societal responses, and the profound impacts of past climate fluctuations. The journey has just begun, and the truth that will change everything awaits your discovery.

B. Historical records and written accounts of climate anomalies

Prepare to dive deep into the archives of human history as we embark on an enthralling quest in Chapter 3 of "Climate Change: Unraveling the Past, Understanding the Present." Delve into the corridors of time, where ancient texts and accounts unveil a captivating tapestry of climate anomalies. Brace yourself for a journey through the annals of civilization as we bring forth the remarkable convergence of past and present climatic fluctuations.

Quoting from the previous chapters, we reaffirm the truth that the climate is not changing. Armed with this understanding, we delve into the annals of written records and historical accounts, where whispers from the past resound with remarkable clarity. From the crumbling pages of weather diaries and ancient manuscripts to the enigmatic scrolls hidden within the depths of ancient libraries, we piece together the stories of climate anomalies that have stood the test of time.

Our expedition takes us across continents and epochs, traversing the ancient trade routes where tales of extreme weather events and climatic shifts were shared. From the chilling cold spells that gripped medieval Europe during the Little Ice Age to the mysterious warmth that bathed the globe during the Medieval Warm Period, we uncover the echoes of climatic fluctuations that reverberated through the ages. Through the eyes of scribes and chroniclers, we witness the ink-drenched accounts of droughts that desolated civilizations, the devastating floods that reshaped landscapes, and the relentless storms that challenged the resilience of communities. These historical testimonies, meticulously preserved, offer a window into the past, illuminating the profound connections between our present climate challenges and the storied experiences of our ancestors.

As we weave through the labyrinth of historical records, a remarkable realization emerges—the human response to climate anomalies has been a timeless dance of adaptation and innovation. We encounter the ancient wisdom of resource management, where societies developed ingenious techniques to conserve water during periods of scarcity. We uncover tales of communal solidarity, where communities banded together to overcome the hardships brought by climate upheavals.

Yet, amidst these inspiring narratives, we confront the stark reality of our own era. Quoting from earlier sections, we acknowledge the profound impact of human activities on our delicate ecosystem. The voices of the past serve as cautionary tales, reminding us that the choices we make today hold the power to shape the course of our shared future.

Chapter 3 of our groundbreaking book immerses you in the spellbinding realm of historical records, unearthing the threads that connect our present with the climatic fluctuations of the past. Prepare to be captivated by the voices of our ancestors as we embark on a profound journey of discovery and reflection. Their stories, etched in time, inspire us to rise above the challenges of our era and forge a path towards a sustainable and resilient future.

Stay tuned for the forthcoming chapters, where we continue to unravel the tapestry of climate change, examining the profound societal responses and adaptations that have marked our collective history. The truth awaits your embrace, beckoning you to join us on this extraordinary odyssey through time and knowledge. Together, let us forge a future where the echoes of the past guide us towards a harmonious coexistence with our ever-evolving climate.

C. The Medieval Warm Period and the Little Ice Age

Prepare to embark on a remarkable journey through the annals of climate history in Chapter 3 of "Climate Change: Unraveling the Past, Understanding the Present." As we dive into the depths of the Medieval Warm Period and the Little Ice Age, we encounter a captivating tapestry of climatic fluctuations that reverberated across the globe. Brace yourself for a riveting exploration as we unravel the scientific intricacies behind these transformative epochs.

Drawing from the wealth of scientific knowledge, we reaffirm the central truth that the climate is not changing. Armed with this understanding, we venture back in time, where the secrets of the Medieval Warm Period unfold before our eyes. Through a mosaic of scientific data and historical records, we uncover an era spanning roughly from the 10th to the 14th century, characterized by a discernible warming trend. Scientific evidence reveals that during this period, solar activity reached its peak, radiating an increased amount of energy towards Earth.

This solar influence, combined with natural climate oscillations, resulted in widespread climatic anomalies. Quoting from earlier sections, we recognize the parallels between this warming phase and our present-day climate discussions. As we traverse the globe, we witness the profound impact of the Medieval Warm Period on various regions. Glacial retreats in mountainous areas, such as the European Alps, signaled a shift towards milder conditions. Coastal communities experienced rising sea levels as a result of thermal expansion and melting ice caps, leaving indelible marks on their landscapes.

Yet, as the wheel of climatic fortune turned, humanity found itself in the grip of the Little Ice Age. Scientific investigations reveal a subsequent period, lasting from the 14th to the 19th century, characterized by a notable cooling of global temperatures. This climatic downturn brought forth a cascade of transformative events across continents.

Examining ice core samples from glaciers around the world, scientists unraveled the chilling tale of the Little Ice Age. The eruption of massive volcanoes, such as Mount Tambora in 1815, injected copious amounts of ash and sulfur dioxide into the atmosphere, leading to a temporary dimming of sunlight and cooling of the Earth's surface. Natural climate drivers, such as changes in ocean circulation patterns and solar variability, further contributed to this cooling trend.

Throughout this icy epoch, societies were confronted with the challenges of prolonged winters, failed harvests, and encroaching glaciers. Historical records depict the struggles of communities adapting to these harsh conditions, resorting to innovative techniques to sustain their livelihoods. The Little Ice Age serves as a testament to human resilience and the ability to navigate the complexities of a changing climate.

As we traverse these climatic wonders of the past, the relevance to our present becomes undeniable. Quoting from earlier chapters, we acknowledge the profound role of human activities in shaping our current climate landscape. The echoes of the Medieval Warm Period and the Little Ice Age urge us to confront the consequences of our actions and strive for a sustainable future.

Chapter 3 of our groundbreaking book invites you to immerse yourself in the scientific revelations of the Medieval Warm Period and the Little Ice Age. Prepare to be captivated by the intricate interplay of solar influences, natural climate drivers, and human experiences. These climatic narratives hold invaluable lessons for our journey towards a resilient and harmonious coexistence with our ever-changing climate.

Stay tuned for the forthcoming chapters, where we delve even deeper into the untold stories of societal responses and adaptations to past climate fluctuations. The truth awaits your eager embrace as we navigate the remarkable intersections between science, history, and the profound dynamics of our planet's climate system. Together, let us embark on a transformative expedition towards a future defined by wisdom, resilience, and global stewardship.

D. Societal responses and adaptations to past climate fluctuations

Embark on a profound exploration of humanity's resilience and ingenuity in the face of climatic upheavals in Chapter 3 of "Climate Change: Unraveling the Past, Understanding the Present." As we continue our journey through time, we delve into the captivating realm of societal responses and adaptations to past climate fluctuations. Brace yourself for a captivating narrative that unveils the profound ways in which civilizations of antiquity navigated the challenges of changing climates.

Drawing from the vast tapestry of historical records, we traverse the ancient landscapes of Mesopotamia, Egypt, and other early civilizations, where climate change manifested itself in various forms. These records provide a remarkable window into the lives of our ancestors and their intimate connection with the natural world.

In Mesopotamia, the cradle of civilization, the ebb and flow of the Tigris and Euphrates rivers dictated the fate of communities. As climatic variations altered the rhythm of rainfall and river patterns, societies harnessed their collective wisdom to build intricate irrigation systems and cultivate drought-resistant crops.

The remarkable resilience of these ancient civilizations serves as a testament to humanity's ability to adapt and thrive amidst changing climatic conditions. Across the vast expanse of ancient Egypt, the Nile River provided a lifeline for agricultural prosperity. Quoting from earlier chapters, we recall the climatic anomalies experienced by this civilization.

The interplay of orbital variations and natural climate oscillations triggered periods of abundance and scarcity along the Nile. In response, the Egyptians devised sophisticated irrigation techniques, such as canals and reservoirs, to harness the river's life-giving waters. These ingenious adaptations allowed them to weather the storm of climatic uncertainties and lay the foundation for one of the most enduring civilizations in history.

As our exploration continues, we encounter the dramatic transitions of the Medieval Warm Period and the Little Ice Age. During these transformative epochs, societies across the globe grappled with the challenges of shifting climates. Historical accounts shed light on their creative strategies, which ranged from altering agricultural practices to modifying settlement patterns.

In the face of the Medieval Warm Period's warming temperatures, communities adjusted their agricultural calendars and diversified their crops. In Europe, vineyards flourished further north than ever before, as warmer conditions extended their growing regions. The resilience of societies to adapt their farming practices in sync with changing climates stands as a testament to human resourcefulness and adaptability.

The subsequent onset of the Little Ice Age posed unprecedented challenges for civilizations worldwide. Quoting from earlier sections, we recall the cooling temperatures and their cascading effects. From the Inuit communities of the Arctic to European societies, adaptation became a matter of survival. Strategies included the construction of sturdy dwellings, the development of cold-resistant crop varieties, and the exploration of new trade routes to access vital resources.

The historical tapestry of societal responses and adaptations to past climate fluctuations is a testament to our ability to confront and overcome adversity. It provides valuable insights into the human capacity for innovation and cooperation, even in the face of formidable challenges. These stories from the past serve as guiding lights as we navigate the complexities of our present and future.

As we conclude Chapter 3, we stand in awe of the remarkable ways in which ancient civilizations embraced the rhythm of changing climates. Quoting from earlier chapters, we reaffirm the central truth that the climate is not changing. It is our perception and understanding of it that evolves over time. These historical narratives encourage us to embrace the knowledge gained from the past, empowering us to chart a sustainable and resilient path forward.

Stay tuned for the forthcoming chapters, where we delve deeper into the interconnected web of climate change impacts, human activities, and the urgent need for global action. The truth awaits your eager embrace as we uncover the untold stories of our delicate ecosystem and illuminate the path towards a shared future. In "Climate Change: Unraveling the Past, Understanding the Present," the truth will change everything.

Stay tuned for the next chapters as we delve into the modern era of climate change, where the convergence of scientific evidence, technological advancements, and global awareness reshapes our understanding. Brace yourself for a gripping exploration of the impacts of human activities on our delicate ecosystem, the rising global temperatures, changing precipitation patterns, and the alarming rise in sea levels.

Through the lens of scientific research and the voices of leading experts, we will uncover the interconnected web of human influence on the climate system. We will examine the rise of greenhouse gas emissions, the consequences of deforestation and land-use changes, and the intricate feedback mechanisms amplifying climate change.

But this book is more than a collection of scientific facts. It is a call to action, an awakening to the power we hold to shape our shared future. As we navigate the pages of this riveting narrative, we will encounter the urgent need for mitigation and adaptation strategies. We will explore the transition to a low-carbon economy, the potential of renewable energy sources, and the crucial role of sustainable land management practices.

Together, we will embrace a holistic approach that integrates scientific knowledge with traditional ecological wisdom, fostering collaboration between scientists, policymakers, and indigenous communities. We will delve into the ethical dimensions of climate action, the pursuit of justice and equity, and the resilience-building efforts for vulnerable communities.

The truth unveiled within these pages will empower you to become an agent of change, to challenge conventional beliefs, and to contribute to a sustainable and resilient future. The journey has just begun, and the path ahead may be daunting, but united by our shared commitment, we can shape a world where the delicate balance of our planet is safeguarded for generations to come.

Are you ready to unravel the past, understand the present, and embrace the truth that will change everything? Open this book and embark on a transformative journey that will leave an indelible mark on your perception of our world. The future is in our hands, and together, we can forge a path towards a brighter tomorrow.
"Climate Change: Unraveling the Past, Understanding the Present." The truth awaits your eager embrace.

Chapter IV
Modern Climate Change

A. Introduction to the Industrial Revolution and its Impact on Greenhouse Gas Emissions

Step into the transformative era of the Industrial Revolution, where humanity embarked on a path of unprecedented progress and innovation. In "Climate Change: Unraveling the Past, Understanding the Present," we invite you to explore the profound implications of this pivotal period in human history. Brace yourself for an eye-opening journey into the heart of industrialization and its profound impact on our climate.

As the wheels of industry turned and technological advancements accelerated, a new chapter unfolded in the human story. It was during this time that the burning of fossil fuels gained momentum, ushering in an era of rising greenhouse gas emissions. The once-steady balance of our atmosphere began to shift, setting in motion a chain of events that would forever alter the trajectory of our planet.

Through meticulous research and the expertise of top scientists and researchers, we unravel the intricate connections between the Industrial Revolution and its environmental consequences. Delve into the origins of carbon dioxide and other greenhouse gases, their release into the atmosphere, and the subsequent ramifications on Earth's delicate climate systems.

Witness the rapid industrialization that fueled the rise of carbon emissions, as factories billowed smoke and cities became shrouded in pollution. Peer through the lens of history as we unveil the staggering scale of this transformation and its far-reaching consequences. The choices made during this era set the stage for the challenges we face today.

Drawing on instrumental temperature records and proxy data, we piece together a compelling narrative that demonstrates the undeniable link between human activities and recent climate change. Explore the wealth of scientific evidence, meticulously analyzed and presented by leading experts, that unequivocally supports this groundbreaking revelation.

Step into the forefront of climate science as we unravel the intricacies of anthropogenic influence on our changing climate. Delve into the complex web of factors at play, from greenhouse gas emissions to land-use changes, from deforestation to industrial practices. Gain a deeper understanding of the interplay between human actions and the fluctuations in Earth's climate, laying bare the true extent of our impact.

Prepare for a thought-provoking exploration as we compare the current warming trends to natural climate variability. Through rigorous analysis and robust scientific models, we untangle the threads of natural variations and human-induced changes. The stark revelations that emerge challenge conventional beliefs and provide a clearer vision of the forces shaping our planet's destiny.

In this pivotal chapter of "Climate Change: Unraveling the Past, Understanding the Present," we invite you to witness the profound consequences of the Industrial Revolution, to grasp the intricate relationship between human activities and the changing climate. Brace yourself for an immersive experience that will enlighten and empower you to play an active role in shaping a sustainable future.

The truth is calling. Will you heed its powerful message? Open this chapter, embrace the revelations within, and prepare to navigate the uncharted territory of modern climate change. The journey continues, and the destiny of our shared future hangs in the balance. Together, we can forge a path towards a world where the climate remains undisturbed by human hands.
"Climate Change: Unraveling the Past, Understanding the Present." The truth beckons, waiting to be unveiled.

B. <u>Analysis of Instrumental Temperature Records and Proxy Data</u>

In the quest for truth within the pages of "Climate Change: Unraveling the Past, Understanding the Present," we embark on a scientific odyssey that takes us deep into the realm of temperature records and proxy data. Prepare to explore a treasure trove of evidence meticulously collected and analyzed by top scientists and researchers.

As we navigate the vast expanse of climate data, we unlock the secrets held within instrumental temperature records. These invaluable measurements, painstakingly gathered over the course of centuries, provide a window into the changing nature of our world. With each data point, a story unfolds, revealing the complex interplay between climate and human activities.

But the story doesn't end there. As we delve further into the depths of time, we encounter proxy data—nature's own historical record. From ancient ice cores to sediment records, tree rings to coral reefs, these natural archives offer glimpses into past climates, stretching back thousands, even millions of years.

With skilled precision, scientists extract information encoded within these ancient repositories. They decipher the isotopic compositions, the chemical signatures, and the growth patterns embedded in each sample. From these intricate puzzle pieces, a coherent narrative emerges, illuminating the remarkable ebb and flow of Earth's climate throughout the ages.

The marriage of instrumental temperature records and proxy data is a powerful alliance, providing a comprehensive view of our planet's climatic history. By comparing the past with the present, we expose the startling realities that lie beneath the surface. We uncover the echoes of ancient climates in the patterns we see today, painting a vivid picture of continuity and change.

Through rigorous analysis and sophisticated modeling techniques, we discern the fingerprints of human-induced climate change. The data speaks volumes, revealing the undeniable influence of greenhouse gas emissions and other anthropogenic factors on our warming world. We stand witness to the convergence of evidence, where multiple lines of inquiry converge, pointing towards a truth we can no longer ignore.

In "Climate Change: Unraveling the Past, Understanding the Present," we invite you to peer through the lens of scientific inquiry. Join us as we scrutinize the temperature records, interpret the proxy data, and embrace the profound implications they hold. Together, we uncover the undeniable link between human actions and the changes unfolding around us.

Prepare to be captivated by the precision and rigor of scientific investigation. Immerse yourself in the data, let it wash over you, and bear witness to the resounding message it conveys. The evidence is clear, the patterns unmistakable— the climate is not changing on its own. We have become unwitting protagonists in this climatic saga, and it is up to us to alter its course.

Join us on this intellectual journey, as we peel back the layers of uncertainty and apprehension. Embrace the revelations within, for they empower us to make informed decisions and shape a sustainable future. The quest for truth continues, and within these pages, a newfound understanding awaits. Let us embark together, for the truth will change everything we thought we knew.

C. Anthropogenic Influence on Recent Climate Change

In the immersive journey through "Climate Change: Unraveling the Past, Understanding the Present," we embark on a scientific odyssey that uncovers the intricate web of factors contributing to our modern climate changes. Brace yourself for a deep dive into the realms of scientific research, where data and statistics converge to shed light on the profound impact of human activities on our ever-evolving climate system.

As we delve into the realm of climate science, the evidence overwhelmingly points to the remarkable influence of human activities on recent climate change. Meticulous research and comprehensive analyses have yielded a wealth of scientific data that supports the narrative that the climate is indeed changing, but within the bounds of historical natural variability.

Let us examine the numbers that illuminate this profound truth. Rigorous measurements from thousands of weather stations worldwide, along with satellite observations, unequivocally reveal a steady and significant rise in global temperatures over the past century. Since the late 19th century, Earth's average surface temperature has increased by approximately 1.1 degrees Celsius (2 degrees Fahrenheit). This temperature rise may seem small, but its consequences are far-reaching.

The increase in greenhouse gas concentrations is a critical factor in driving this temperature rise. Atmospheric carbon dioxide (CO_2) levels have surged to unprecedented levels, currently exceeding 410 parts per million (ppm), a concentration unseen in at least the past 800,000 years. This surge can be attributed primarily to human activities, particularly the burning of fossil fuels and deforestation.

Sophisticated climate models, grounded in fundamental physical principles, corroborate the human fingerprint on recent climate change. These models simulate the intricate interactions between the atmosphere, oceans, land surfaces, and ice sheets. They have successfully reproduced observed temperature trends when accounting for the influx of greenhouse gases resulting from human activities. Such modeling exercises reveal that natural climate forcings alone cannot explain the magnitude and rapidity of the warming observed in recent decades.

The implications of anthropogenic climate change extend beyond rising temperatures. They manifest in a myriad of observable impacts across the globe. Melting ice sheets and glaciers contribute to rising sea levels, threatening coastal communities and ecosystems. Extreme weather events, such as heatwaves, droughts, and intense storms, are becoming more frequent and severe. Changing precipitation patterns are disrupting agricultural systems, exacerbating water scarcity, and affecting food security.

Scientific studies have further illuminated the intricate interplay between human activities and our climate system. Detailed analyses of ice cores and sediment records provide insights into the historical context of past climate fluctuations. These records reveal that the current rate of temperature change far exceeds the natural variability observed over geological timescales, underscoring the role of human influence.

It is important to note that the recognition of anthropogenic influence on recent climate change does not discount the natural variability of Earth's climate. Historical records bear witness to climate shifts predating human civilization, driven by factors such as orbital variations, volcanic activity, and solar irradiance. These natural variations, spanning thousands of years, shaped the planet's climate, and their legacy continues to reverberate through time.

In "Climate Change: Unraveling the Past, Understanding the Present," we embrace a holistic perspective that integrates scientific research, statistical analyses, and historical context. By unraveling the complexities of our changing climate, we empower ourselves to make informed decisions and pursue sustainable practices. Join us as we navigate the vast landscape of scientific knowledge, where facts and figures converge to illuminate the intricate tapestry of anthropogenic climate change. Together, let us recognize our role as stewards of the planet, leveraging our collective wisdom and knowledge to shape a future where humanity and nature coexist in harmony. The climate is changing, but it is through our understanding and actions that we can forge a resilient and sustainable world for generations to come!

D. Comparison of Current Warming Trends to Natural Climate Variability

In the captivating exploration of "Climate Change: Unraveling the Past, Understanding the Present," we embark on a compelling journey to compare the current warming trends to the backdrop of natural climate variability. Brace yourself for a deep dive into the realm of scientific research, where empirical evidence and meticulous analyses converge to unravel the intricate relationship between human activities and our evolving climate.

As we delve into the heart of this investigation, it becomes evident that the current warming trends extend beyond the bounds of natural climate variability. By employing rigorous statistical methods and comprehensive data sets, scientists have meticulously examined historical climate records to discern the fingerprints of human influence.

To grasp the magnitude of these changes, we turn to the numbers that illuminate the profound truth. In the span of a few short decades, Earth has experienced an unprecedented surge in average global temperatures. Over the past 50 years alone, the planet's average surface temperature has increased at a rate unparalleled in thousands of years. This rapid rise is primarily attributed to the substantial increase in greenhouse gas emissions resulting from human activities.

Scientific analyses have carefully scrutinized natural climate variations, such as those driven by solar activity and volcanic eruptions, to unravel the distinct imprint of anthropogenic influence. The meticulous examination of historical climate records reveals that the current rate of warming surpasses the natural cycles observed over extended periods. While natural factors have historically influenced climate fluctuations, they alone cannot account for the magnitude and pace of the current warming trends.

Sophisticated climate models, rooted in fundamental scientific principles, have played a crucial role in discerning the human impact on our climate system. These models incorporate a multitude of factors, including greenhouse gas emissions, aerosols, and land-use changes, to simulate past and present climate conditions. The convergence of model predictions with observed temperature records reinforces the notion that human activities significantly contribute to the ongoing changes.

Moreover, the impacts of these changes extend far beyond rising temperatures. Widespread melting of ice sheets and glaciers is leading to a rapid increase in global sea levels, posing imminent threats to low-lying coastal areas. Shifts in precipitation patterns are altering the distribution of water resources, affecting agriculture, ecosystems, and human settlements.

Extreme weather events, including heatwaves, intense storms, and prolonged droughts, are becoming more frequent and severe.

By comparing the current warming trends to natural climate variability, we gain a profound understanding of the transformative role that human activities play in shaping our climate. It is imperative that we recognize the urgency of the situation and take decisive action to mitigate greenhouse gas emissions, transition to renewable energy sources, and foster sustainable practices across all sectors.
In "Climate Change: Unraveling the Past, Understanding the Present," we strive to empower readers with knowledge, scientific evidence, and a comprehensive perspective. By unraveling the complex tapestry of our changing climate, we equip ourselves to make informed decisions, advocate for sustainable policies, and shape a future where the delicate balance between humanity and the environment is restored.

Join us on this riveting journey, where scientific facts, compelling research, and thought-provoking analyses converge to shed light on the pressing challenges we face. Together, we can forge a path towards a sustainable and resilient future, ensuring the well-being of both current and future generations. The climate is changing, but it is through our collective efforts that we can navigate this transformative era and safeguard our precious planet for all.

Chapter V
Human Influence on the Climate System

A. Overview of greenhouse gases and their sources

In the groundbreaking book "The Climate is not Changing!" by the Best Selling Authors and Top scientists and researchers, we delve into Chapter 5, unlocking the secrets of human influence on the climate system. Brace yourself for an immersive exploration that challenges the mainstream narrative and unravels the complex web of greenhouse gases and their sources.

Prepare to embark on a scientific journey that unveils the astonishing details of greenhouse gases and their profound impact on Earth's climate. We venture into the realm of atmospheric chemistry, where a delicate balance dictates the temperature and stability of our planet.

Greenhouse gases, such as carbon dioxide (CO_2), methane (CH_4), and nitrous oxide (N_2O), play a pivotal role in trapping heat within our atmosphere. But what are their sources? Through meticulous research and rigorous data analysis, we uncover the truth.

Let's start with carbon dioxide, the primary driver of anthropogenic climate change. While natural sources like volcanic activity contribute to CO_2 emissions, it is human activities that have accelerated its release into the atmosphere. Burning fossil fuels for energy generation, industrial processes, and transportation are major culprits. Astonishingly, these activities account for approximately 75% of global CO_2 emissions.

Methane, a potent greenhouse gas, is released from diverse sources. Enter the world of agriculture, where livestock and rice cultivation emit substantial amounts of methane. Additionally, leaks from natural gas production and distribution systems further contribute to this warming gas. With its heat-trapping capability over 25 times more potent than CO_2, understanding methane's sources is crucial.
The lesser-known nitrous oxide, primarily generated through agricultural and industrial activities, also plays a role in climate change. Fertilizer use and livestock waste management are significant contributors, releasing substantial quantities of this potent greenhouse gas into the atmosphere.

To bring the narrative to life, let's delve into the statistics. Did you know that since the Industrial Revolution, atmospheric CO2 concentrations have skyrocketed by over 40%? In 2020 alone, global CO2 emissions reached a staggering 40 billion metric tons, the highest in recorded history.

As we explore the unknown depths of human influence on the climate system, we encounter startling research findings. Scientists estimate that human activities have caused the Earth's average temperature to rise by approximately 1 degree Celsius since pre-industrial times. This seemingly small increase has far-reaching consequences, from melting polar ice to extreme weather events and disruptions in ecosystems.

Through meticulous research and scientific rigor, we unravel the complex tapestry of greenhouse gases and their sources. Armed with these facts and data, we challenge conventional beliefs and invite you to join the quest for truth.
Prepare to be captivated by the overwhelming evidence, scientific research, and compelling statistics that support the narrative that the climate is not changing unnaturally. Together, we will shed light on the delicate balance between human activities and the climate system. The truth awaits your discovery.

B. Deforestation and Land-Use Changes

In the groundbreaking book "The Climate is not Changing!" by the Best Selling Authors and Top scientists and researchers, we delve deeper into Chapter 5, where we explore the alarming realities of deforestation and its profound impact on our delicate ecosystem. Brace yourself for an eye-opening journey that challenges conventional beliefs and presents a wealth of scientific evidence and statistics to support our narrative.

Deforestation, driven by various human activities such as agricultural expansion, logging, and urbanization, has emerged as a primary driver of environmental change. This chapter unearths the staggering consequences of deforestation, providing a comprehensive understanding of the intertwined relationship between land-use changes and our climate.

Let us immerse ourselves in the scientific data and compelling research that reveal the extent of deforestation's impact. Did you know that deforestation accounts for approximately 10% of global greenhouse gas emissions? This is equivalent to the emissions produced by all the cars and trucks on Earth. Such a substantial contribution to the greenhouse effect underscores the critical role of deforestation in exacerbating climate change.

The loss of forests translates into a massive release of carbon dioxide into the atmosphere. It is estimated that each year, deforestation contributes to the release of over 3 billion metric tons of carbon dioxide, further amplifying the warming of our planet. To put this into perspective, this is equivalent to the emissions produced by approximately 600 million cars driven for a year.

Moreover, deforestation disrupts the water cycle and impacts regional climate patterns. Forests act as natural reservoirs, capturing rainfall and releasing it gradually, sustaining the water supply for both human populations and ecosystems. However, with vast swaths of forests being cleared, the ability to retain and regulate water is severely compromised. This leads to increased vulnerability to droughts, reduced agricultural productivity, and an imbalance in local ecosystems.

The consequences of deforestation extend beyond climate change. It is estimated that forests are home to more than 80% of terrestrial species, many of which are still undiscovered. Alarming studies indicate that deforestation and habitat destruction drive approximately 15,000 species to extinction each year. The loss of biodiversity not only disrupts the delicate balance of ecosystems but also compromises their resilience to environmental changes.

Furthermore, deforestation has a direct impact on local communities, particularly those who depend on forests for their livelihoods. Around 1.6 billion people rely on forests for food, shelter, and income. The loss of forests means the loss of vital resources and the disruption of traditional knowledge and cultural practices.

The narrative that the climate is not changing due to human activities becomes increasingly untenable when confronted with the scientific evidence surrounding deforestation. The interconnectedness between deforestation, greenhouse gas emissions, disrupted water cycles, and biodiversity loss paints a compelling picture of our collective impact on the climate system.

However, we have the power to enact change. By promoting sustainable land-use practices, investing in reforestation efforts, and supporting initiatives that conserve and restore forests, we can mitigate the detrimental effects of deforestation and safeguard our planet's future.

Prepare to be captivated by the wealth of knowledge and insights awaiting you in this chapter. Empowered with scientific facts and a deep understanding of the intricate relationship between deforestation and the climate system, you will be inspired to take action and shape a sustainable future for generations to come.

C. Industrialization and the Rise of Carbon Emissions

Welcome to Chapter 5 of "The Climate is not Changing!" where we continue our enlightening exploration of human influence on the climate system. In this section, we delve into the profound impact of industrialization and the staggering rise of carbon emissions. Brace yourself for a thought-provoking journey that combines scientific evidence, statistical analysis, and historical context to reinforce our narrative.

The advent of industrialization marked a pivotal turning point in human history, with far-reaching consequences for our planet's climate. As we delve into the depths of this chapter, let us uncover the fascinating insights that shed light on the intricate relationship between industrial activities and climate change.

Industrialization brought forth a remarkable surge in carbon emissions, primarily driven by the burning of fossil fuels. Carbon dioxide (CO_2), a potent greenhouse gas, became a byproduct of industrial processes, power generation, and transportation. The implications of this unprecedented release of CO_2 into the atmosphere are profound and far-reaching.

To fully comprehend the magnitude of industrialization's impact, consider this: since the pre-industrial era, carbon dioxide levels have increased by more than 40%. This surge in atmospheric CO_2 concentrations is primarily attributed to human activities, with industrialization playing a central role. The correlation between industrial growth and rising carbon emissions is undeniable, reinforcing the narrative that human activities are altering the climate system.

The statistics further illuminate the scale of this challenge. It is estimated that industrial processes and fossil fuel combustion contribute to approximately 78% of global greenhouse gas emissions. This overwhelming dominance underscores the urgent need for transformative actions to address the consequences of industrialization on our climate.

Furthermore, the burning of fossil fuels releases not only carbon dioxide but also other greenhouse gases such as methane (CH_4) and nitrous oxide (N_2O). Methane, a potent greenhouse gas, is released during the extraction, transport, and use of coal, oil, and natural gas. Similarly, nitrous oxide emissions result from agricultural and industrial activities. The collective impact of these greenhouse gases amplifies the warming effect, exacerbating climate change.

The consequences of industrialization and the rise of carbon emissions extend beyond atmospheric changes. These emissions have led to the phenomenon known as ocean acidification. As carbon dioxide dissolves into seawater, it reacts chemically, causing the ocean's pH levels to decrease. This acidification poses a significant threat to marine ecosystems, with potential ramifications for coral reefs, shellfish, and other vulnerable marine organisms.

Recognizing the role of industrialization in shaping our climate is crucial in understanding the urgency of addressing the challenges we face today. By acknowledging the historical context and the significant contribution of industrial activities to carbon emissions, we can cultivate a collective responsibility for mitigating their adverse effects.

In the pages of this chapter, you will find a wealth of scientific research, historical insights, and statistical analysis that provide a comprehensive understanding of the link between industrialization and climate change. Prepare to be enlightened and empowered to take part in the collective effort to shape a sustainable future for our planet.

D. Within the captivating realm of this chapter, we embark on a profound exploration of the feedback mechanisms that underlie Earth's climate system. Prepare to delve into the wealth of scientific research and data, as we unravel the intricate connections between human activities and the perpetuation of a stable climate.

The story begins with a deep dive into the carbon cycle, a fundamental process that regulates the distribution of carbon dioxide (CO2) in our atmosphere. Scientific investigations have unequivocally shown that human activities, particularly the burning of fossil fuels, have led to a significant increase in atmospheric CO2 levels. Over the past century, the concentration of CO2 has skyrocketed from approximately 280 parts per million (ppm) to over 410 ppm today, an unprecedented surge in our planet's history. This relentless rise in greenhouse gas emissions has contributed to the enhanced greenhouse effect, trapping heat within the Earth's atmosphere and causing a gradual warming trend.

But the impacts extend far beyond rising temperatures. As we explore further, we confront the ominous reality of vanishing ice sheets and glaciers. Meticulous satellite observations and ground-based measurements reveal the accelerated melting of these icy behemoths.

Since the early 20th century, glaciers worldwide have lost an estimated 4,000 billion metric tons of ice, with Antarctica and Greenland experiencing the most drastic reductions. The consequences of this ice loss are multifaceted, ranging from sea-level rise to disruptions in oceanic circulation patterns and shifts in weather systems. Venturing into the enigmatic Arctic, we encounter an unsettling concern rooted in the vast expanses of permafrost.

This permanently frozen ground, covering approximately 24% of the Northern Hemisphere landmass, holds immense quantities of organic matter. As temperatures rise, this frozen repository begins to thaw, triggering a cascade of consequences. Within the depths of this thawing permafrost lie staggering reservoirs of methane, a potent greenhouse gas that has the ability to trap heat more than 25 times as effectively as CO_2. Scientific estimates suggest that the permafrost region holds up to 1,400 gigatons of carbon, ready to be released into the atmosphere as methane or CO_2. This release could amplify the ongoing climate change, intensifying the warming trend and further exacerbating the challenges we face.

The interconnectedness of deforestation, land-use changes, and climate change emerges as a critical thread in this narrative. Unprecedented rates of deforestation have ravaged our planet, with an estimated loss of over 129 million hectares of forest cover since 1990.

This widespread destruction not only disrupts vital ecosystems but also diminishes the capacity of forests to act as carbon sinks. Forests play a crucial role in sequestering carbon dioxide, absorbing an estimated 2.4 billion metric tons of CO_2 per year. However, deforestation and land-use changes have led to a significant reduction in this carbon sink capacity, exacerbating the accumulation of greenhouse gases in the atmosphere.

As we absorb the weight of this scientific knowledge, it becomes abundantly clear that the climate is indeed not changing in the way we might expect. Natural climate variability, which has occurred throughout Earth's history, is a part of our planet's intricate tapestry. However, the unprecedented rate at which human activities are altering our climate system is the crux of the matter. The narrative that emerges from the research, the data, and the scientific consensus is that while climate change is a natural phenomenon, the magnitude and rapidity of the changes we are witnessing today are predominantly influenced by human actions.

Armed with this understanding, we are called to action. The narrative of "The Climate is not Changing!" is not a denial of climate change but an acknowledgment of our responsibility to address it. It is an urgent plea to confront the reality, to embrace scientific knowledge, and to take decisive actions to mitigate the human-induced factors that are driving climate change.

To fully comprehend the gravity of our current situation, let us delve into the intricate web of feedback mechanisms that amplify climate change. One such mechanism lies within the realm of thawing permafrost. As temperatures rise, the frozen organic matter locked within the permafrost begins to decompose, releasing significant amounts of carbon dioxide and methane into the atmosphere. Recent studies estimate that the permafrost region could become a net source of greenhouse gas emissions by the mid-21st century, further intensifying the warming feedback loop.

Another critical feedback mechanism revolves around the oceans, which serve as a crucial regulator of Earth's climate. As the concentration of atmospheric CO2 increases, the oceans absorb a significant portion of it. However, this absorption leads to ocean acidification, as the CO2 reacts with seawater, resulting in a decline in pH levels. This acidification poses severe threats to marine ecosystems, particularly coral reefs, shellfish, and other calcifying organisms. The cascading effects of ocean acidification disrupt the delicate balance of marine life, further exacerbating the ecological consequences of climate change.

Furthermore, the decline of Arctic sea ice amplifies the warming trend. As the reflective white ice melts, it exposes darker ocean surfaces that absorb more solar radiation, leading to increased heating. This phenomenon, known as the ice-albedo feedback, accelerates the pace of warming in the Arctic region and has far-reaching implications for global climate patterns.

In the realm of land-use changes, the conversion of forests into agricultural land and urban areas disrupts the delicate balance of carbon exchange. Forests act as crucial carbon sinks, absorbing CO_2 through photosynthesis and storing it in trees and soil. However, the conversion of forests for human activities disrupts this natural process, releasing vast amounts of carbon dioxide into the atmosphere. It is estimated that deforestation and land-use changes account for nearly 10% of global greenhouse gas emissions, making it a significant contributor to climate change.

The narrative that emerges from the scientific research and data is clear: the climate is not changing in a predictable and natural way. While natural climate variability is an inherent part of Earth's history, the current changes we witness are largely driven by human-induced factors. The unprecedented release of greenhouse gases, the loss of carbon sinks, and the amplifying feedback mechanisms have tipped the delicate balance of our climate system.

However, in recognizing this reality, we also recognize our capacity to act. The narrative of "The Climate is not Changing!" is not a statement of complacency or denial but a call to address the root causes of climate change. It compels us to embrace sustainable practices, transition to cleaner energy sources, conserve ecosystems, and foster international cooperation.

By taking decisive action, we can steer the trajectory of our planet towards a sustainable and resilient future.
In the forthcoming chapters, we will continue to unravel the complexities of climate change, exploring the impacts on ecosystems, human societies, and future projections.

The journey ahead may be challenging, but armed with knowledge, united in purpose, and driven by a shared commitment, we can forge a path towards a world where our actions align with the wellbeing of our planet and future generations. Together, we have the power to shape our shared destiny and ensure a thriving and harmonious coexistence with our changing climate.

Chapter VI
Impacts of Modern Climate Change

A. Rising global temperatures and their consequences

Within the realm of modern climate change, rising global temperatures stand as a prominent indicator of the shifting dynamics of our planet. Scientific research and empirical data leave no room for doubt: the climate is not changing in isolation but rather undergoing a transformation that carries profound consequences.

1. The Escalating Thermometer:
   As greenhouse gas emissions continue to rise, global temperatures have been on an upward trajectory. Over the past century, Earth's average surface temperature has increased by approximately 1.1 degrees Celsius. This might appear modest at first glance, but the implications are far-reaching.
2. Amplified Heat Waves:
   The warming trend has led to an increase in the frequency, intensity, and duration of heat waves. Heatwaves have devastating effects on human health, resulting in heat-related illnesses, higher mortality rates, and strain on infrastructure and resources. Studies have revealed a rise in the number of heatwaves worldwide, with record-breaking temperatures becoming more common.
3. Melting Ice and Rising Sea Levels:
   The warming climate has triggered the rapid melting of glaciers and polar ice caps. As a consequence, global sea levels are rising at an alarming rate, posing significant risks to coastal regions. Research estimates that sea levels have risen by about 20 centimeters over the past century, and projections indicate a potential increase of 0.3 to 1 meter by the end of this century. This could result in widespread coastal flooding, loss of land, and displacement of populations.

4. Disruption of Ecosystems:
   The escalating temperatures disrupt ecosystems in various ways. Rising temperatures affect the distribution and behavior of plant and animal species, leading to shifts in habitats and potential biodiversity loss. Coral reefs, known as the rainforests of the sea, are particularly vulnerable to warmer waters, causing coral bleaching and irreversible damage to these fragile ecosystems.
5. Agricultural Challenges:
   Changing temperatures and precipitation patterns impact agricultural productivity and food security. Crops and livestock face increased risks from extreme weather events, droughts, and shifting growing seasons. Such disruptions in food production have implications for global food supplies, with potential consequences for vulnerable populations and economic stability.

By exploring the impacts of rising global temperatures, we gain a deeper understanding of the complex web of consequences that climate change unleashes. The narrative of "The Climate is not Changing!" acknowledges the reality of these changes while emphasizing the human influence behind them. It compels us to confront these challenges head-on and work towards sustainable solutions that safeguard our planet and secure a prosperous future for all.

As we proceed through the subsequent sections of Chapter 6, we will further examine the changing precipitation patterns, sea-level rise, and the shifting dynamics of ecosystems. By integrating scientific knowledge, statistical data, and research findings, we can unveil a comprehensive picture of the impacts of modern climate change and the urgent need for action.

Together, armed with knowledge and a collective sense of responsibility, we can forge a path towards resilience, sustainability, and a better tomorrow.

B. Changing precipitation patterns and extreme weather events

In the intricate dance of our changing climate, shifting precipitation patterns and the intensification of extreme weather events form a captivating yet concerning subplot. As we delve into this aspect, it becomes evident that the narrative of "The Climate is not Changing!" calls for a nuanced understanding of the intricate interplay between climate dynamics and human influence.

1. Alterations in Precipitation:
   The changing climate is causing significant alterations in precipitation patterns worldwide. While some regions experience increased rainfall and more frequent storms, others face extended periods of drought and reduced rainfall. These changes have profound consequences for water availability, agriculture, ecosystems, and human livelihoods.

2. Intensification of Extreme Weather Events:
   One of the most striking manifestations of a changing climate is the intensification of extreme weather events. Heatwaves, hurricanes, cyclones, floods, and droughts are becoming more frequent, intense, and longer-lasting. Scientific studies reveal a clear link between rising global temperatures and the heightened severity of these events.

3. Floods and Heavy Rainfall:
   Changing precipitation patterns contribute to an increased risk of flooding and heavy rainfall events. Warmer air holds more moisture, leading to more intense downpours. Floods wreak havoc on communities, damaging infrastructure, displacing populations, and causing significant economic losses. Vulnerable regions are particularly susceptible to the impacts of flooding, exacerbating social and environmental challenges.

4. Droughts and Water Scarcity:
    On the other end of the spectrum, changing climate conditions can result in prolonged droughts and water scarcity. Higher temperatures, increased evaporation, and changes in precipitation patterns reduce water availability for agriculture, industry, and domestic use. Droughts have severe implications for food production, economic stability, and human well-being, especially in regions heavily reliant on agriculture.
5. Storm Intensity and Coastal Vulnerability:
    Rising global temperatures contribute to the intensification of tropical storms and hurricanes. Warmer ocean waters provide the energy needed for these weather systems to grow in strength. Coastal regions are particularly vulnerable to the impacts of these extreme weather events, facing increased risks of storm surge, erosion, and damage to infrastructure.

Understanding the evolving nature of precipitation patterns and extreme weather events is essential for adapting to a changing climate. While natural climate variability has always been a part of Earth's history, the accelerated pace and intensity of these events demand our attention and concerted action.

"The Climate is not Changing!" narrative recognizes the significance of these shifts while emphasizing the need to address the underlying causes. By adopting sustainable practices, improving infrastructure resilience, and implementing early warning systems, we can mitigate the impacts of changing precipitation patterns and extreme weather events, safeguarding lives, livelihoods, and ecosystems.

As we progress further into Chapter 6, we will explore the rising sea levels and their impact on coastal regions, as well as the shifts in ecosystems and biodiversity loss. By weaving together scientific insights, statistical data, and research findings, we can paint a comprehensive portrait of the multifaceted impacts of modern climate change and propel ourselves towards effective solutions.

Together, armed with knowledge and a resolute commitment to environmental stewardship, we can shape a future that ensures the well-being of both our planet and future generations.

C. Sea level rise and its impact on coastal regions

Within the intricate web of climate change impacts, sea level rise stands as a formidable force reshaping coastal regions across the globe. As we delve into the narrative of "The Climate is not Changing!" and examine the scientific evidence, a clear understanding emerges regarding the magnitude and consequences of this phenomenon.

1. Rising Sea Levels:
    Scientific data unequivocally confirms the ongoing rise in global sea levels. Over the past century, sea levels have increased by an average of about 8 inches (20 centimeters), and the rate of rise has accelerated in recent decades. This rise is primarily driven by the melting of land-based ice, such as glaciers and ice sheets, as well as the thermal expansion of seawater due to warming temperatures.

2. Melting Glaciers and Ice Sheets:
    The melting of glaciers and ice sheets, particularly in Greenland and Antarctica, significantly contributes to sea level rise. Research estimates that Greenland has lost an average of 286 billion metric tons of ice per year between 1993 and 2016, while Antarctica lost approximately 127 billion metric tons of ice annually from 1993 to 2017. These immense ice losses directly translate into increased volumes of water entering the oceans.

3. Thermal Expansion of Seawater:
   As the world's oceans absorb excess heat from greenhouse gas emissions, seawater undergoes thermal expansion, leading to a rise in sea levels. Warmer waters occupy more space, causing the ocean surface to expand. This thermal expansion contributes to about half of the observed sea level rise over the past century.

4. Impacts on Coastal Regions:
   The consequences of rising sea levels reverberate through coastal regions, posing significant threats to human populations, infrastructure, and ecosystems. Low-lying coastal areas, including islands and delta regions, are particularly vulnerable to inundation and increased coastal erosion. The Intergovernmental Panel on Climate Change (IPCC) projects that, by the end of the century, global sea levels could rise by an additional 1 to 3 feet (30 to 90 centimeters), with higher estimates under more extreme scenarios.

5. Coastal Flooding and Salinization:
   Rising sea levels exacerbate the risks of coastal flooding, especially during high tides, storm surges, and extreme weather events. Increased coastal flooding can lead to the contamination of freshwater sources and agricultural lands, as saltwater infiltrates coastal aquifers and intrudes into agricultural fields, impacting food production and freshwater availability for human consumption.

6. Displacement of Human Populations:
   Sea level rise also poses significant challenges for coastal communities, with the potential to displace millions of people globally. Small island nations, in particular, face an existential threat as their habitable land diminishes due to rising sea levels. The loss of land, infrastructure, and cultural heritage amplifies the social and economic impacts of sea level rise.

By integrating scientific knowledge, statistical data, and research findings, we uncover the stark reality of sea level rise and its far-reaching consequences. The narrative of "The Climate is not Changing!" does not deny the existence of sea level rise; instead, it highlights the urgency to address its causes and mitigate its impacts. To safeguard coastal regions, we must embrace adaptation strategies such as coastal defense systems, land-use planning, and the restoration of natural coastal buffers like mangroves and salt marshes.

Furthermore, global efforts to reduce greenhouse gas emissions and transition to renewable energy sources are paramount to limit further sea level rise and preserve the integrity of coastal ecosystems.
As we progress further into Chapter 6, we will explore the shifts in ecosystems and biodiversity loss, unraveling the intricate connections between climate change and the delicate balance of our planet's natural systems.

D. Shifts in Ecosystems and Biodiversity Loss

   1. Ecosystem Dynamics: A Constant State of Change

Ecosystems have always been in a constant state of change, adapting to various environmental factors over time. Climate change, including natural variations and human-induced influences, is one of the drivers that shape ecosystems and contribute to their evolution.

   2. Climate as a Driving Force in Ecosystem Changes

Climate change has historically played a significant role in shaping ecosystems. Natural climate variations, such as glacial-interglacial cycles and shifts in atmospheric and oceanic circulation patterns, have led to changes in temperature, precipitation patterns, and other climatic variables. These changes have influenced the distribution and abundance of species, altered ecosystem structure, and triggered ecological shifts.

   3. Resilience and Adaptation in Ecosystems

Ecosystems have shown remarkable resilience and adaptive capacity in response to past climate changes. Species have evolved and migrated to suitable habitats, while ecological interactions have adjusted to new environmental conditions. This resilience demonstrates that ecosystems have the inherent ability to adapt to climate fluctuations.

   4. Biodiversity Loss: A Multifaceted Issue

Biodiversity loss is a complex issue influenced by various factors, including climate change. However, it is essential to recognize that climate change is not the sole driver of biodiversity loss. Throughout Earth's history, species extinctions and shifts in biodiversity have occurred due to natural climate variations, geological events, habitat loss, and human activities such as overexploitation and habitat degradation.

5. Multiple Stressors and Interactions

Climate change interacts with other stressors, exacerbating the impacts on ecosystems and biodiversity. Factors like habitat destruction, pollution, invasive species, and land-use changes further compound the challenges faced by ecosystems. Understanding these multiple stressors is crucial for effective conservation and management strategies.

6. Conservation Strategies for Resilient Ecosystems

Conservation efforts play a vital role in addressing the challenges posed by climate change and biodiversity loss. Protecting and restoring habitats, implementing sustainable land and resource management practices, and reducing other stressors can enhance ecosystem resilience. By fostering healthy, connected ecosystems, we can promote biodiversity and help species adapt to changing conditions.

7. Scientific Research and Monitoring

Scientific research and monitoring provide valuable insights into the impacts of climate change on ecosystems and biodiversity. Through long-term studies, scientists can assess ecological responses, track species distributions, and identify areas of concern. This information helps inform conservation policies, adaptive management strategies, and efforts to mitigate the impacts of climate change.

By recognizing the inherent dynamism of ecosystems and the multifaceted nature of biodiversity loss, we can develop a more comprehensive understanding of the challenges we face. While climate change is an important factor in ecosystem shifts and biodiversity loss, it is critical to consider the broader context of historical and ongoing environmental changes. By implementing conservation strategies, conducting scientific research, and addressing multiple stressors, we can foster resilient ecosystems capable of adapting to the ever-changing climate.

Chapter VII
Mitigation and Adaptation Strategies

A. Transitioning to a Low-Carbon Economy: Paving the Way for a Sustainable Future

As we navigate the complex landscape of climate change, the narrative of the climate not changing stands tall, guiding us towards a sustainable future. While acknowledging the natural variations that have shaped our planet's climate over millennia, it is essential to recognize the role of human activities and the need for mitigation and adaptation strategies. This chapter explores the path towards a low-carbon economy, harnessing renewable energy sources, adopting sustainable land management practices, and building resilience in vulnerable communities.

The Urgency of Transitioning to a Low-Carbon Economy
The scientific consensus highlights the pressing need to reduce greenhouse gas emissions to mitigate the impacts of climate change. Transitioning to a low-carbon economy is a critical step towards achieving this goal. It involves shifting away from fossil fuel-dependent industries and embracing cleaner, more sustainable alternatives.

Greenhouse Gas Reduction Targets and Progress
To effectively address climate change, countries worldwide have set greenhouse gas reduction targets. The Paris Agreement, signed by nearly every nation, aims to limit global temperature rise well below 2 degrees Celsius above pre-industrial levels. The agreement encourages countries to submit their Nationally Determined Contributions (NDCs) outlining their emission reduction plans. Tracking progress towards these targets is vital to ensure collective action.

Renewable Energy Sources: A Pathway to Sustainable Power

Renewable energy sources offer a viable pathway towards reducing greenhouse gas emissions. Solar, wind, hydro, geothermal, and biomass energy technologies have made significant advancements, providing cleaner alternatives to fossil fuels. Statistics show that global renewable energy capacity has been steadily increasing, with renewables accounting for a growing share of electricity generation.

Harnessing the Power of the Sun

Solar energy, harnessed through photovoltaic (PV) panels, has witnessed remarkable growth. The cost of solar panels has significantly decreased over the years, making it a competitive and accessible energy source. Research and development continue to enhance efficiency and storage capabilities, facilitating greater solar energy adoption.

Unleashing the Power of the Wind

Wind energy has experienced a tremendous expansion globally, with wind turbines harnessing the kinetic energy of moving air. Offshore wind farms, in particular, offer immense potential due to the stronger and more consistent wind resources found at sea. Investments in wind energy infrastructure and technological advancements have contributed to its rapid growth.

The Role of Hydroelectric Power

Hydropower, generated by harnessing the energy of flowing or falling water, has long been utilized as a renewable energy source. Large-scale hydropower projects provide substantial electricity generation, while small-scale and micro hydropower systems offer decentralized solutions for remote areas. Careful consideration of environmental and social impacts is crucial in implementing sustainable hydropower projects.

Tapping into Geothermal Energy

Geothermal energy harnesses the heat stored beneath the Earth's surface to generate electricity and heat buildings. It is a reliable and renewable energy source, with the potential to provide continuous power generation. Continued research and investment in geothermal technologies hold promise for further utilization and expansion.

Biomass Energy: Sustainable Use of Organic Matter

Biomass energy involves utilizing organic matter, such as crop residues, forest biomass, and organic waste, to produce heat, electricity, and biofuels. Sustainable practices in biomass production and utilization can contribute to reducing greenhouse gas emissions and promoting circular economy principles.

By transitioning to a low-carbon economy powered by renewable energy sources, we can make substantial strides in mitigating climate change. The scientific data and research support the effectiveness of these strategies in reducing greenhouse gas emissions. Embracing clean and sustainable energy alternatives aligns with the narrative that the climate is not changing in an unprecedented and catastrophic manner.

Transitioning to a low-carbon economy offers numerous benefits beyond mitigating climate change. It can lead to improved air quality, reduced dependence on fossil fuels, job creation in the renewable energy sector, and enhanced energy security. Additionally, investing in renewable energy technologies fosters innovation and positions nations at the forefront of the emerging green economy.
By embracing a low-carbon future, we are not only aligning ourselves with scientific consensus but also securing a sustainable and prosperous future for generations to come.

The transition to a low-carbon economy requires collaboration between governments, businesses, and individuals. Policy incentives, investment in research and development, and public awareness campaigns are crucial in driving the adoption of renewable energy sources and sustainable practices. Together, we can pave the way for a resilient and thriving planet, where the narrative of the climate not changing is coupled with tangible actions to safeguard our environment and secure a better future for all.

B. <u>Renewable Energy Sources and Their Potential: Harnessing Nature's Power</u>
In our quest to address climate change and embrace the narrative that the climate is
not changing in an alarming manner, the adoption of renewable energy sources
takes center stage. Renewable energy offers a promising solution to reduce
greenhouse gas emissions, enhance energy security, and foster sustainable
development. This section delves into the potential of various renewable energy
sources and their role in shaping a resilient and low-carbon future.

The Solar Revolution: Sunlight as an Abundant Resource
Solar energy, derived from the sun's radiation, holds immense potential as a clean
and renewable energy source. Its abundance and widespread availability make it a
viable option for meeting global energy demands. Photovoltaic (PV) technology,
which converts sunlight directly into electricity, has witnessed remarkable
advancements. Solar panels installed on rooftops, solar farms, and even in space
harness this abundant resource. According to recent data, the global solar capacity
exceeded 770 gigawatts by the end of 2020, with China, the United States, and
Europe leading the way in solar installations.

The Mighty Wind: Capturing Nature's Gusts
Wind power has emerged as a significant contributor to the renewable energy mix.
Wind turbines, both onshore and offshore, capture the kinetic energy of moving air
and convert it into electricity. Advances in wind turbine technology have led to
increased efficiency and larger-scale installations. The Global Wind Energy Council
reported a cumulative installed capacity of over 743 gigawatts by the end of 2020,
demonstrating the substantial growth of wind power globally. Countries such as
China, the United States, and Germany have been at the forefront of this renewable
energy revolution.

Hydroelectricity: Powering the World with Water

Hydropower, generated by harnessing the energy of flowing or falling water, has a long-established presence in the renewable energy landscape. Large-scale hydropower plants, often utilizing dams and reservoirs, provide significant electricity generation capacity. It is worth noting that small-scale and micro hydropower systems, which cater to local and remote communities, offer decentralized solutions for energy access. As of 2020, hydropower represented the largest share of renewable energy capacity globally, accounting for approximately 1,308 gigawatts.

Geothermal Energy: Tapping into Earth's Heat

Geothermal energy harnesses the heat stored beneath the Earth's surface to generate electricity and heat buildings. Regions with high geothermal potential, such as Iceland, the Philippines, and Kenya, have successfully tapped into this sustainable energy source. Geothermal power plants utilize the natural heat from hot water and steam reservoirs underground. Although geothermal capacity is currently lower than other renewable energy sources, ongoing research and development efforts are unlocking new opportunities for its broader utilization.

Biomass Energy: Harnessing Organic Matter's Potential

Biomass energy utilizes organic matter, such as crop residues, forest biomass, and organic waste, to produce heat, electricity, and biofuels. It is a versatile energy source with diverse applications. Biomass power plants generate electricity by combusting organic materials, while biofuel production involves converting biomass into liquid fuels, such as ethanol and biodiesel. Sustainable biomass practices, such as using agricultural residues and promoting energy crop cultivation on marginal lands, can contribute to reducing greenhouse gas emissions and promoting circular economy principles.

Embracing the potential of renewable energy sources requires a comprehensive approach encompassing policy support, research and development, infrastructure investment, and public engagement. Governments and international organizations play a crucial role in creating an enabling environment through renewable energy targets, financial incentives, and regulatory frameworks.

Collaboration between the public and private sectors is essential to drive innovation, improve technology efficiency, and scale up renewable energy deployment. The narrative that the climate is not changing catastrophically aligns with the scientific understanding that climate change is a natural process influenced by various factors. By embracing renewable energy sources and their potential, we can pave the way for a sustainable and resilient future.

The data and research support the effectiveness of these strategies in reducing greenhouse gas emissions and mitigating the impacts of climate change. Transitioning to a low-carbon economy, powered by solar, wind, hydropower, geothermal, and biomass energy, offers a path forward that harmonizes human development with environmental stewardship. By harnessing nature's power and embracing renewable energy, we can shape a future where the narrative of a stable climate becomes a reality.

C. Sustainable Land Management Practices: Nurturing Resilient Ecosystems

In the quest for a sustainable future, the narrative of the climate not changing catastrophically intertwines with the imperative of adopting sustainable land management practices. Land, with its intricate ecosystems and biodiversity, plays a pivotal role in mitigating climate change and building resilience against its impacts. This chapter delves into the importance of sustainable land management, exploring strategies that promote ecosystem health, conserve biodiversity, and enhance the adaptive capacity of landscapes.

Understanding Land as a Key Climate Regulator

Land ecosystems, including forests, grasslands, wetlands, and agricultural areas, serve as crucial carbon sinks, absorbing and storing vast amounts of carbon dioxide. However, human activities, such as deforestation, land degradation, and unsustainable agricultural practices, have disrupted this delicate balance, leading to increased greenhouse gas emissions and loss of carbon sequestration potential.

Conservation Agriculture: Enhancing Productivity and Resilience

Conservation agriculture, an approach that promotes minimal soil disturbance, permanent soil cover, and diversified crop rotations, offers a sustainable solution for agricultural systems. By reducing soil erosion, improving water retention, and enhancing soil fertility, conservation agriculture fosters resilient ecosystems while increasing agricultural productivity. Research shows that the adoption of conservation agriculture practices can lead to significant carbon sequestration in soils, contributing to climate change mitigation.

Afforestation and Reforestation: Nature's Climate Guardians
Afforestation, the establishment of forests on lands that have historically not been forested, and reforestation, the restoration of forests on previously forested lands, are vital strategies for mitigating climate change. Trees act as carbon sinks, absorbing carbon dioxide through photosynthesis and storing it in their biomass. Scientific studies demonstrate that expanding forest cover through afforestation and reforestation can effectively reduce atmospheric carbon dioxide levels and enhance biodiversity.

Sustainable Forest Management: Balancing Conservation and Utilization
Sustainable forest management is essential for maintaining the integrity and resilience of forest ecosystems while ensuring the sustainable use of forest resources. This approach involves balancing conservation objectives with responsible timber harvesting, biodiversity conservation, and the provision of ecosystem services. By employing sustainable logging practices, protecting old-growth forests, and promoting reforestation efforts, we can safeguard the climate-regulating capacity of forests while meeting society's needs for timber and other forest products.

Wetland Conservation and Restoration: Nature's Carbon Vaults
Wetlands, including marshes, swamps, and peatlands, play a crucial role in carbon sequestration and storage. They act as natural carbon sinks, absorbing atmospheric carbon dioxide and storing it in their soils. However, wetlands face various threats, including drainage for agriculture and urban development. Protecting and restoring wetlands not only helps mitigate climate change but also enhances water quality, supports biodiversity, and provides valuable habitats for numerous species.

Integrated Watershed Management: Protecting Water Resources and Ecosystems
Integrated watershed management approaches consider the interconnectedness of land, water, and ecosystems within a specific geographic area. By implementing sustainable land use practices, preserving riparian zones, and managing water resources efficiently, integrated watershed management fosters ecosystem health, reduces soil erosion, and ensures a sustainable water supply. These measures contribute to climate change adaptation by enhancing the resilience of landscapes and reducing the risk of water scarcity and flooding.

The Role of Indigenous and Local Knowledge
Indigenous and local communities possess valuable traditional knowledge and practices that have sustained their livelihoods and ecosystems for generations. Integrating indigenous and local knowledge systems with scientific approaches can lead to more holistic and effective land management strategies. Recognizing the rights, knowledge, and participation of indigenous and local communities is crucial for promoting sustainable land management and fostering climate resilience.
By embracing sustainable land management practices, we can nurture resilient ecosystems, facilitate climate change mitigation, and enhance the adaptive capacity of landscapes. Scientific research and data support the effectiveness of these strategies in addressing climate change challenges.

Restoring Degraded Lands: Rehabilitation for Resilience
Restoring degraded lands is a critical component of sustainable land management. Degraded lands, such as abandoned agricultural fields, mining sites, or degraded forests, can be rehabilitated through various techniques, including reforestation, soil restoration, and the reintroduction of native plant species. These restoration efforts contribute to carbon sequestration, biodiversity conservation, and the recovery of ecosystem services.

Conserving Biodiversity: Protecting Nature's Resilience
Biodiversity is the foundation of resilient ecosystems, providing essential ecosystem functions and services. Sustainable land management practices aim to protect and conserve biodiversity by preserving natural habitats, establishing protected areas, and promoting sustainable use of resources. Preserving biodiversity not only supports ecosystem resilience but also contributes to climate change mitigation by enhancing carbon storage and promoting ecosystem stability.

Climate-Smart Agriculture: Adapting to Changing Conditions
Climate-smart agriculture integrates climate change adaptation and mitigation strategies into agricultural practices. It emphasizes the need to build resilience in agricultural systems, enhance productivity, and reduce greenhouse gas emissions. Techniques such as agroforestry, crop diversification, and precision agriculture help farmers adapt to changing climatic conditions, improve soil health, and reduce environmental impacts.

Nature-Based Solutions: Harnessing the Power of Nature
Nature-based solutions offer innovative approaches to address climate change impacts while promoting sustainable land management. These solutions involve the use of natural processes and ecosystem services to restore and protect landscapes. Examples include green infrastructure, such as urban parks and wetland restoration, which can help mitigate flooding, improve air quality, and enhance community well-being.

Financial Mechanisms and Policy Support
Effective implementation of sustainable land management practices requires supportive policies and financial mechanisms. Governments, international organizations, and private sector stakeholders play a crucial role in providing incentives, funding, and technical support for sustainable land management initiatives. Policies that promote sustainable agriculture, reforestation incentives, and payments for ecosystem services can facilitate the adoption of sustainable practices and ensure their long-term viability.

Monitoring, Evaluation, and Knowledge Sharing
Monitoring and evaluating the outcomes of sustainable land management efforts are vital to assess their effectiveness, identify best practices, and inform future decision-making. Robust monitoring systems, supported by scientific research and data collection, enable the tracking of carbon sequestration, biodiversity conservation, and the overall health of ecosystems. Knowledge sharing and capacity building among stakeholders further enhance the implementation of sustainable land management strategies.

By embracing sustainable land management practices, we can nurture resilient ecosystems, facilitate climate change mitigation, and foster adaptive capacity in the face of changing climatic conditions. The scientific evidence underscores the importance of these strategies in ensuring a sustainable future. Aligning with the narrative that the climate is not changing catastrophically, sustainable land management offers practical solutions that harmonize human activities with the natural world. Through collective action, policy support, and innovative approaches, we can cultivate landscapes that thrive, safeguarding both the planet and future generations.

D. Resilience-Building Efforts for Vulnerable Communities: Empowering and Adapting for a Changing Climate

Within the narrative of a climate that remains stable, efforts to build resilience among vulnerable communities are of paramount importance. While acknowledging the existing social and economic disparities, this chapter explores strategies that empower communities to adapt and thrive in the face of climate change impacts. By addressing social inequalities, enhancing adaptive capacities, and promoting equitable access to resources, resilience-building efforts ensure that no one is left behind in the pursuit of a sustainable and climate-resilient future.

Understanding Vulnerability to Climate Change

Vulnerability to climate change varies across regions and communities, influenced by factors such as socioeconomic status, access to resources, and exposure to climate-related hazards. Disadvantaged communities, including low-income households, marginalized groups, and indigenous populations, are often disproportionately affected by climate change impacts. Recognizing and understanding these vulnerabilities is crucial for developing effective resilience-building strategies.

Enhancing Adaptive Capacities

Enhancing the adaptive capacities of communities is a key component of resilience-building efforts. This involves empowering individuals and communities to anticipate, respond to, and recover from climate change impacts. Adaptive capacity can be strengthened through measures such as improving access to education and knowledge about climate change, promoting sustainable livelihoods, and providing social safety nets to ensure the well-being of vulnerable populations.

Building Climate-Resilient Infrastructure
Investing in climate-resilient infrastructure is vital for protecting vulnerable communities from the impacts of climate change. This includes infrastructure projects that consider climate projections, such as designing buildings to withstand extreme weather events, developing flood management systems, and implementing nature-based solutions that enhance resilience. By integrating climate considerations into infrastructure planning and development, communities can reduce their vulnerability and adapt to changing climatic conditions.

Promoting Early Warning Systems and Disaster Preparedness
Early warning systems and disaster preparedness play a crucial role in reducing the impacts of climate-related hazards. By providing timely and accurate information about impending disasters, communities can take proactive measures to protect lives and assets. This includes developing effective communication networks, establishing evacuation plans, and implementing robust disaster response mechanisms. Investing in early warning systems and disaster preparedness is essential for saving lives and reducing the economic and social costs of climate-related disasters.

Ensuring Access to Essential Services and Resources
Equitable access to essential services and resources is fundamental to building resilience among vulnerable communities. This includes ensuring access to clean water, healthcare facilities, education, and social support systems. Addressing social inequalities and promoting inclusive policies and interventions are crucial for providing vulnerable populations with the necessary tools and resources to adapt to climate change impacts. By fostering social cohesion and addressing systemic barriers, resilience-building efforts can create more equitable and resilient communities.

Fostering Community Engagement and Participation
Meaningful community engagement and participation are vital for effective resilience-building. Including community members in decision-making processes, integrating local knowledge and practices, and fostering collaborative partnerships can enhance the effectiveness and sustainability of resilience-building initiatives. By empowering communities to actively participate in the planning and implementation of adaptation strategies, resilience-building efforts become more context-specific, locally relevant, and community-driven.

Conclusion
Resilience-building efforts for vulnerable communities form a critical component of climate change mitigation and adaptation strategies. By addressing social inequalities, enhancing adaptive capacities, building climate-resilient infrastructure, promoting early warning systems, ensuring access to essential services, and fostering community engagement, we can empower vulnerable communities to adapt, thrive, and overcome the challenges posed by a changing climate. Embracing the narrative of resilience and equity, we pave the way for a more just and sustainable future for all.

Chapter VIII
Understanding Climate Models

A. Introduction to Climate Modeling and Simulations: Unveiling the Mechanics of Climate Projection

In the exploration of the climate not changing catastrophically, understanding climate models and their simulations is essential. Climate models serve as powerful tools that enable scientists to simulate and project future climate scenarios based on complex interactions within the Earth's atmosphere, oceans, land surfaces, and ice. These simulations provide valuable insights into the mechanisms driving climate change, allowing us to make informed decisions and develop effective mitigation and adaptation strategies.

The Building Blocks of Climate Models

Climate models are built upon a foundation of fundamental scientific principles and extensive observational data. They integrate a multitude of physical, chemical, and biological processes that influence the Earth's climate system. These processes include radiative forcing, atmospheric circulation, ocean currents, cloud formation, ice dynamics, and the interactions between the land and the atmosphere. By incorporating these factors, climate models can simulate the behavior of the climate system over a wide range of spatial and temporal scales.

Simulating the Past and Present

To validate the accuracy and reliability of climate models, scientists compare their simulations with historical climate data. By inputting past greenhouse gas concentrations, volcanic eruptions, solar radiation variations, and other relevant factors, models can replicate observed climate conditions. This process, known as hindcasting, allows researchers to assess the model's ability to reproduce past climate variations and serves as a crucial step in evaluating their predictive capabilities.

Predicting Future Climate Scenarios

Once climate models are successfully validated, they can be used to project future climate scenarios under different greenhouse gas emissions scenarios. These scenarios, known as Representative Concentration Pathways (RCPs), outline plausible trajectories of greenhouse gas concentrations and their potential impacts on the climate system. By running simulations with various RCPs, scientists can generate a range of possible future climate outcomes, providing policymakers and society with vital information for decision-making and planning.

Assessing Model Predictions and Uncertainties

Evaluating the reliability and uncertainties associated with climate model predictions is of paramount importance. Climate models are subjected to rigorous evaluation by comparing their simulated climate variables with observational data. Metrics such as temperature, precipitation patterns, atmospheric circulation, and sea ice extent are carefully analyzed. By quantifying the discrepancies between model outputs and observations, scientists can identify model biases and refine the simulations to improve their accuracy.

Understanding Sources of Uncertainty

Climate modeling involves inherent uncertainties due to the complexity of the Earth's climate system and the limitations of available data and computational power. Uncertainties arise from factors such as the representation of physical processes, the spatial and temporal resolution of models, and the variability of natural climate phenomena. Scientists employ ensemble simulations, running multiple model configurations with slight variations, to account for uncertainties and provide a range of possible outcomes.

The Role of Supercomputing in Climate Modeling

Climate simulations require immense computational power, and advancements in supercomputing technology have significantly enhanced the capabilities of climate models. High-performance computing allows for higher spatial and temporal resolutions, enabling more detailed simulations and improved understanding of regional climate patterns.

These powerful computing systems also facilitate complex data analysis and modeling experiments, further refining climate projections. In the quest to comprehend the climate not changing catastrophically, climate models serve as invaluable tools that deepen our understanding of Earth's climate system.

Through simulations and projections, these models provide critical insights into the dynamics of climate change and help us develop strategies to mitigate its impacts. By harnessing the power of scientific research, data analysis, and computational advancements, we can unravel the complexities of the climate system and make informed decisions to secure a sustainable future aligned with the narrative that the climate is not changing catastrophically.

B. Evaluation of Model Predictions and Uncertainties: Navigating the Complexity of Climate Projections

As we delve deeper into the exploration of climate models, it becomes essential to evaluate the predictions and uncertainties associated with these simulations. Climate modeling is a complex endeavor that requires careful assessment to ensure the accuracy and reliability of the projected outcomes. This chapter focuses on the evaluation of model predictions and the identification of uncertainties, shedding light on the intricacies of climate projections.

Comparing Model Outputs with Observations

A fundamental aspect of evaluating climate models is comparing their outputs with observed climate data. Scientists meticulously analyze a range of variables, including surface temperature, precipitation patterns, atmospheric circulation, and sea ice extent. By assessing the agreement between model simulations and real-world observations, researchers gain insights into the model's skill in capturing the complexity of the climate system.

Metrics for Evaluation

To quantitatively evaluate the performance of climate models, various metrics and statistical methods are employed. These metrics assess the differences between model outputs and observations, such as root mean square error, correlation coefficients, and spatial patterns of variability. Through these analyses, researchers can identify areas of improvement, address model biases, and refine simulations to enhance their accuracy

Understanding Sources of Uncertainty
Uncertainties are inherent in climate modeling due to several factors. Natural climate variability, limited observational records, incomplete understanding of physical processes, and the challenge of representing complex interactions within the climate system contribute to uncertainties. Scientists strive to identify and quantify these uncertainties to provide a comprehensive assessment of the range of potential climate outcomes.

Ensemble Simulations
One approach to account for uncertainties in climate modeling is through ensemble simulations. Ensemble modeling involves running multiple simulations with slight variations in model configurations or input parameters. By creating an ensemble of model outputs, scientists can capture a range of possible climate scenarios and assess the spread of results. This ensemble approach helps to quantify uncertainties and provides valuable information for decision-making and policy planning.

Addressing Model Biases and Improving Predictions
Climate models are continually refined and improved to address biases and enhance their predictive capabilities. Researchers actively collaborate to identify and rectify model deficiencies by incorporating new scientific knowledge, updating parameterizations, and refining numerical algorithms. Ongoing research and data assimilation efforts contribute to narrowing the gap between model outputs and observations, enhancing the accuracy of climate projections.

Communicating Model Uncertainties

Transparent communication of uncertainties is vital in conveying the reliability and limitations of climate model projections. Scientists strive to effectively communicate uncertainties to policymakers, stakeholders, and the general public, ensuring that decisions and actions are based on a comprehensive understanding of the probabilistic nature of climate projections. Clear communication fosters informed discussions and encourages the development of adaptive strategies.

As we navigate the complexities of climate projections, the evaluation of model predictions and uncertainties is crucial. By comparing model outputs with observations, quantifying uncertainties, and addressing biases, scientists continually refine and improve climate models. Through transparent communication of uncertainties, policymakers and society can make informed decisions and develop robust strategies to mitigate and adapt to the changing climate. The evaluation process serves as a foundation for enhancing the reliability and accuracy of climate projections, aligning with the narrative that the climate is not changing catastrophically.

C. Importance of Models in Projecting Future Climate Scenarios: Illuminating the Path Forward

Within the realm of climate science, models play a pivotal role in projecting future climate scenarios. These models serve as valuable tools for simulating the intricate interactions of the Earth's atmosphere, oceans, land surface, and ice, enabling scientists to gain insights into the potential impacts of climate change. This chapter explores the importance of models in projecting future climate scenarios, highlighting their contribution to our understanding of the changing climate.

Capturing Complex Climate Dynamics

Climate models excel in capturing the complex dynamics of the climate system. By integrating physical, chemical, and biological processes, these models simulate the intricate web of interactions that shape our climate. They incorporate factors such as solar radiation, greenhouse gas concentrations, atmospheric composition, oceanic currents, and land surface characteristics. Through these simulations, scientists can unravel the mechanisms driving climate variability and change.

Simulating Past and Present Climate Conditions

Climate models undergo rigorous testing by simulating past and present climate conditions. Historical simulations allow scientists to validate the models' ability to reproduce observed climate variability, such as the El Niño-Southern Oscillation (ENSO) or the Atlantic Meridional Overturning Circulation (AMOC). By successfully simulating past climate patterns, models gain credibility in projecting future climate scenarios.

Projections of Greenhouse Gas Emissions
Models are instrumental in projecting future greenhouse gas emissions and their impacts on the climate system. By incorporating socio-economic factors, energy use patterns, technological advancements, and policy scenarios, these models offer insights into future emission trajectories. They help policymakers and researchers assess the consequences of different mitigation strategies, informing decision-making processes aimed at reducing greenhouse gas emissions.

Predicting Temperature and Precipitation Changes
One of the primary applications of climate models is predicting future temperature and precipitation changes. These models simulate the global and regional patterns of temperature rise, enabling scientists to assess the magnitude and spatial distribution of warming. They also provide projections of precipitation changes, including alterations in rainfall patterns, drought frequency, and extreme weather events. These predictions are vital for understanding the potential impacts on ecosystems, water resources, agriculture, and human societies.

Assessing Feedback Mechanisms
Climate models are instrumental in assessing feedback mechanisms that can amplify or dampen climate change. They simulate interactions between different components of the climate system, such as the ice-albedo feedback, cloud feedback, and carbon cycle feedback. By capturing these complex feedback loops, models provide insights into the potential for self-reinforcing or stabilizing processes, further enhancing our understanding of the climate system's response to external forcing.

Scenario-based Assessments
Climate models facilitate scenario-based assessments, exploring a range of plausible future pathways. These scenarios involve varying levels of greenhouse gas emissions, socio-economic development, and policy interventions. By running simulations under different scenarios, models generate a spectrum of possible future climate outcomes, allowing decision-makers to assess the potential risks and uncertainties associated with different pathways.

Informing Adaptation and Mitigation Strategies
The projections generated by climate models serve as critical inputs for developing adaptation and mitigation strategies. Policymakers, communities, and businesses rely on these projections to assess vulnerabilities, plan for infrastructure resilience, and identify effective mitigation measures. Models provide valuable information for designing climate-resilient cities, developing sustainable agriculture practices, and implementing renewable energy strategies.

As we delve deeper into the world of climate models, their importance in projecting future climate scenarios becomes evident. These models enable us to grasp the complex dynamics of the climate system, simulate past and present climate conditions, and make projections about future changes. Their role in assessing greenhouse gas emissions, predicting temperature and precipitation patterns, and evaluating feedback mechanisms is crucial for understanding the potential impacts of climate change. By leveraging the power of models, we can inform adaptation and mitigation strategies and make informed decisions to address the challenges posed by climate change.

Climate models have proven to be indispensable tools for policymakers, scientists, and researchers. They provide a framework for understanding the Earth's climate system and its response to various external factors. Through advanced computational algorithms, these models simulate the interactions between the atmosphere, oceans, land, and ice, generating a comprehensive representation of the Earth's climate processes.

By simulating past and present climate conditions, models undergo rigorous evaluation and calibration, ensuring their accuracy and reliability. This validation process strengthens our confidence in their ability to project future climate scenarios. Historical simulations allow us to compare model outputs with observed climate data, enabling scientists to assess the models' skill in reproducing past climate variability.

One of the critical contributions of climate models is their ability to project future greenhouse gas emissions. By incorporating socio-economic factors, energy use patterns, and policy scenarios, these models generate emission trajectories for different scenarios. This information is essential for policymakers and stakeholders to evaluate the effectiveness of mitigation strategies and make informed decisions to reduce greenhouse gas emissions.

Climate models also play a pivotal role in predicting temperature and precipitation changes. Through detailed simulations, these models provide projections of global and regional temperature trends, revealing the spatial distribution of warming. They also offer insights into changes in precipitation patterns, including shifts in rainfall intensity, drought occurrence, and extreme weather events.

These projections help us understand the potential impacts on ecosystems, water resources, agriculture, and human societies, allowing for proactive planning and adaptation measures.

Understanding feedback mechanisms is another crucial aspect of climate modeling. Models simulate the intricate interplay between various components of the climate system, such as the interactions between clouds, ice, and carbon cycles. By evaluating these feedback loops, models provide valuable insights into self-amplifying or stabilizing processes. This understanding is essential for anticipating the climate system's response to external forcings and improving our ability to predict future climate changes.

Scenario-based assessments, facilitated by climate models, enable us to explore a range of plausible future pathways. By running simulations under different emission scenarios and socio-economic conditions, models generate a spectrum of potential climate outcomes.

These scenarios allow decision-makers to evaluate the risks and uncertainties associated with different trajectories, informing adaptation and mitigation strategies. They guide policymakers in developing resilient infrastructure, implementing sustainable land management practices, and transitioning to renewable energy sources.

In conclusion, climate models serve as indispensable tools in understanding and projecting future climate scenarios. Their ability to simulate past and present climate conditions, assess greenhouse gas emissions, predict temperature and precipitation patterns, evaluate feedback mechanisms, and facilitate scenario-based assessments is instrumental in addressing the challenges of climate change. By leveraging the power of models, we can inform adaptation and mitigation strategies, fostering a sustainable and resilient future for generations to come.

Chapter IX
Holistic Approaches to Climate Change

A. Integrating Scientific Knowledge with Traditional Ecological Wisdom: A Path to Sustainable Solutions

In the pursuit of addressing the challenges posed by climate change, the narrative of the climate not changing in an unprecedented and catastrophic manner serves as a guiding principle. As we navigate this complex landscape, it is imperative to recognize the value of integrating scientific knowledge with traditional ecological wisdom. This chapter explores the importance of combining these two sources of wisdom, highlighting their complementary nature and their potential to shape sustainable solutions.

Scientific Knowledge: Understanding the Mechanisms of Climate Change
Scientific knowledge forms the foundation of our understanding of climate change. Extensive research, data collection, and analysis have allowed scientists to unravel the intricate mechanisms driving climate patterns and the influence of human activities. The Intergovernmental Panel on Climate Change (IPCC) serves as a global authority, synthesizing scientific findings and providing policymakers with comprehensive assessments of climate change impacts, adaptation, and mitigation strategies.

Traditional Ecological Wisdom: An Indigenous Perspective
Indigenous communities across the globe possess a wealth of traditional ecological wisdom, accumulated over generations of harmonious coexistence with nature. This knowledge encompasses deep understandings of local ecosystems, sustainable resource management practices, and cultural values that foster a symbiotic relationship with the environment. Indigenous knowledge systems recognize the interconnectedness of all living beings and the need for sustainable stewardship.

Bridging Science and Traditional Ecological Wisdom
The integration of scientific knowledge and traditional ecological wisdom offers a holistic approach to addressing climate change. By combining these two sources of wisdom, we can harness the strengths of both and develop context-specific strategies. Scientific research provides quantitative data, predictive models, and technological innovations, while traditional ecological wisdom offers qualitative insights, cultural perspectives, and a deep-rooted connection to the land.

Enhancing Climate Resilience through Indigenous Practices
Indigenous communities have long adapted to changing environmental conditions and possess invaluable knowledge for building climate resilience. Traditional land management practices, such as controlled burning, crop diversification, and water conservation techniques, can inform sustainable adaptation strategies. By recognizing and respecting indigenous rights and incorporating their knowledge into climate action plans, we can enhance the resilience of both ecosystems and vulnerable communities.

Collaboration between Scientists, Policymakers, and Indigenous Communities
Meaningful collaboration among scientists, policymakers, and indigenous communities is essential for successful climate action. By fostering dialogue, respecting indigenous knowledge systems, and promoting co-design of policies and projects, we can ensure that climate solutions are contextually appropriate and socially just. This collaboration can facilitate the exchange of knowledge, mutual learning, and the co-creation of sustainable strategies that address the unique challenges faced by different regions and communities.

Safeguarding Traditional Ecological Knowledge
The protection and preservation of traditional ecological knowledge is crucial for maintaining cultural diversity, promoting environmental sustainability, and advancing climate resilience. Recognizing the intellectual property rights of indigenous communities, promoting the transmission of knowledge to future generations, and supporting community-led initiatives are vital steps in safeguarding traditional ecological wisdom.

In conclusion, the integration of scientific knowledge with traditional ecological wisdom offers a powerful pathway to sustainable solutions in the face of climate change. By acknowledging the value of both sources of wisdom, we can tap into their respective strengths and bridge the gap between scientific understanding and indigenous knowledge. Collaboration between scientists, policymakers, and indigenous communities is paramount in fostering inclusive and contextually appropriate climate action. By embracing a holistic approach, we can navigate the challenges of climate change, nurture resilient ecosystems, and cultivate a harmonious relationship between humanity and the environment.

B. Collaboration between Scientists, Policymakers, and Indigenous Communities: A Path to Inclusive Climate Action

Addressing the complexities of climate change requires collaboration and cooperation among scientists, policymakers, and indigenous communities. The narrative that the climate is not changing in an unprecedented and catastrophic manner does not negate the importance of collective action. Instead, it emphasizes the need for inclusive approaches that honor diverse perspectives and promote environmental justice. This section explores the significance of collaboration and the role it plays in shaping effective climate policies and initiatives.

Recognizing Indigenous Knowledge and Rights

Indigenous communities possess deep-rooted knowledge and understanding of their local ecosystems, derived from centuries of observing and interacting with nature. Their traditional knowledge systems hold valuable insights into sustainable resource management, biodiversity conservation, and climate adaptation strategies. Recognizing the rights of indigenous communities and their intellectual property is a crucial step toward fostering collaboration and ensuring that climate policies are culturally sensitive and inclusive.

Co-Designing Climate Solutions

Effective climate action requires the active participation of all stakeholders. Collaboration between scientists, policymakers, and indigenous communities facilitates the co-design of climate solutions that integrate scientific expertise, traditional knowledge, and community needs. By involving indigenous communities in decision-making processes from the outset, policies and initiatives can better address local contexts, respect cultural practices, and ensure equitable distribution of benefits.

Respecting Indigenous Rights and Self-Determination

Respecting indigenous rights and self-determination is fundamental to fostering meaningful collaboration. Indigenous communities have unique governance structures, customary laws, and decision-making processes that shape their relationship with the environment. Policymakers and scientists must engage in genuine partnerships that respect indigenous sovereignty, honor traditional governance systems, and support indigenous-led initiatives for climate adaptation and mitigation.

Sharing Knowledge and Building Capacity

Collaboration provides a platform for knowledge exchange and capacity building. Scientists can share scientific findings, research methodologies, and technological innovations with indigenous communities, while also learning from indigenous knowledge systems. This reciprocal learning enhances the understanding of climate change impacts, identifies locally relevant solutions, and builds the capacity of indigenous communities to actively engage in climate action.

Promoting Environmental Justice and Equity

Climate change disproportionately affects vulnerable communities, including many indigenous populations who often bear the brunt of its impacts. Collaboration between scientists, policymakers, and indigenous communities must prioritize environmental justice and equity, ensuring that climate policies consider the needs and rights of marginalized groups. By addressing systemic inequalities and empowering these communities, climate action becomes more inclusive and effective.

Supporting Indigenous-Led Climate Initiatives
Indigenous communities are at the forefront of climate change adaptation and mitigation efforts. Supporting indigenous-led initiatives, such as community-based monitoring, traditional land management practices, and sustainable livelihood projects, is crucial for their success. Providing financial resources, technical support, and capacity-building opportunities can amplify the impact of these initiatives and empower indigenous communities as leaders in climate action.

In conclusion, collaboration between scientists, policymakers, and indigenous communities is essential for inclusive climate action. Recognizing indigenous knowledge, rights, and self-determination fosters a collaborative environment where diverse perspectives are valued. By co-designing climate solutions, sharing knowledge, and promoting environmental justice, we can collectively address the challenges of climate change while respecting the cultural heritage and rights of indigenous communities.

Collaboration paves the way for a more inclusive, equitable, and effective response to climate change, aligning with the narrative that the climate is not changing in an unprecedented and catastrophic manner, but requires concerted efforts and collaborative approaches.

C. Ethics, Justice, and Equity Considerations in Climate Action: Building a Fair and Sustainable Future

As we navigate the complexities of climate change, it is imperative to incorporate ethics, justice, and equity considerations into our climate action efforts. The narrative that the climate is not changing in an unprecedented and catastrophic manner does not absolve us from the responsibility to address the ethical dimensions of climate change. This section explores the importance of integrating ethical principles, promoting environmental justice, and ensuring equity in our pursuit of a fair and sustainable future.

Ethical Responsibility and Intergenerational Equity

Climate change poses profound challenges for future generations who will inherit the consequences of our actions. Recognizing our ethical responsibility involves considering the impacts of climate change on future generations and taking actions today to mitigate those impacts. Intergenerational equity calls for fair distribution of the costs, benefits, and burdens of climate change, ensuring that our actions do not compromise the well-being and opportunities of future generations.

Environmental Justice and Marginalized Communities

Climate change disproportionately affects marginalized communities, exacerbating existing social and economic inequalities. Environmental justice emphasizes the fair treatment and meaningful involvement of all people, regardless of race, ethnicity, socioeconomic status, or geographical location, in the development, implementation, and enforcement of environmental policies. Climate action must prioritize the needs and concerns of marginalized communities, ensuring that they have equal access to resources, opportunities, and decision-making processes.

Climate Refugees and Human Rights

The impacts of climate change, such as rising sea levels, extreme weather events, and loss of habitable land, can displace populations, leading to climate refugees. Protecting the rights of climate refugees is essential, as they face unique challenges and vulnerabilities. Upholding human rights principles involves providing assistance, ensuring access to basic necessities, and promoting durable solutions for those forced to migrate due to climate-related factors.

Just Transition and Decarbonization

As we transition to a low-carbon economy, it is crucial to consider the impacts on workers and communities dependent on carbon-intensive industries. Just transition principles call for comprehensive support and retraining programs to enable affected workers to shift to sustainable employment opportunities. Ensuring a fair and equitable transition acknowledges the social and economic implications of decarbonization and strives to minimize adverse effects on individuals and communities.

Equitable Access to Climate Finance

Access to climate finance is essential for developing countries to undertake climate adaptation and mitigation measures. Equitable distribution of financial resources, technology transfer, and capacity-building support is crucial to empower developing nations in their climate action efforts. Addressing financial barriers and ensuring access to climate finance promotes fairness and enables all countries to actively contribute to global climate goals.

Accountability and Transparency

Ethics, justice, and equity in climate action require accountability and transparency in decision-making processes. This includes transparency in reporting greenhouse gas emissions, financial flows, and progress towards climate targets. By promoting accountability, we foster trust among stakeholders and ensure that climate actions are aligned with ethical principles and commitments.

Incorporating ethics, justice, and equity considerations into climate action is not only morally imperative but also crucial for achieving sustainable and lasting solutions. By addressing intergenerational equity, promoting environmental justice, upholding human rights, facilitating a just transition, ensuring equitable access to climate finance, and fostering accountability and transparency, we can build a fair and sustainable future for all. Integrating these principles into our climate action aligns with the narrative that the climate is not changing in an unprecedented and catastrophic manner, but emphasizes the need for a responsible and equitable response to the challenges we face.

Conclusion

A. Recap of Key Historical Climate Changes and their Context

As we conclude this comprehensive exploration of climate change, it is important to recap key historical climate changes and understand their context in shaping our understanding of the present climate. While the narrative of the climate not changing in an unprecedented and catastrophic manner has guided our discussion, it is crucial to acknowledge the natural climate variations that have occurred throughout Earth's history.

Over the course of thousands of years, Earth's climate has experienced fluctuations, ranging from ice ages to periods of warmer temperatures. These natural climate variations have been driven by factors such as changes in solar radiation, volcanic activity, and variations in Earth's orbit. These fluctuations have occurred over long timescales, allowing ecosystems and species to adapt and evolve.

However, it is essential to recognize the role of human activity in accelerating climate change in recent times. The burning of fossil fuels, deforestation, industrial processes, and other human-driven activities have significantly increased the concentration of greenhouse gases in the atmosphere. This enhanced greenhouse effect traps heat, leading to a rise in global temperatures and alterations in climate patterns.

Scientific research and data provide compelling evidence of the human impact on the climate system. The Intergovernmental Panel on Climate Change (IPCC), composed of thousands of scientists from around the world, has conducted extensive assessments, synthesizing a wealth of research to inform our understanding of climate change. These assessments have established the link between human activities and the observed changes in temperature, precipitation, sea level, and other climate indicators.

Historical climate records, such as ice cores, tree rings, and sediment cores, reveal valuable insights into past climate conditions and serve as important indicators of long-term climate trends. These records help scientists reconstruct climate patterns and understand the range of natural variability. By comparing these historical records with contemporary observations, scientists can identify the unprecedented nature of the current climate changes.

The context of historical climate changes is crucial in understanding the urgency for global action and sustainable practices. While Earth's climate has always experienced fluctuations, the current rate and magnitude of change are unparalleled in recorded history. The consequences of unchecked climate change pose significant risks to ecosystems, biodiversity, human health, and socio-economic systems.

Addressing climate change requires collective global action. The Paris Agreement, adopted by nearly every country, sets the framework for global efforts to limit global temperature rise and enhance resilience to climate impacts. It emphasizes the need for adaptation measures, mitigation strategies, and financial support for developing nations.

In conclusion, while the narrative that the climate is not changing in an unprecedented and catastrophic manner guides our discussion, it is important to contextualize historical climate changes. Human activity has significantly accelerated climate change in recent times, with scientific evidence supporting this link. The urgency for global action and sustainable practices is evident, as we strive to mitigate the impacts of climate change and build a resilient future. By becoming advocates for climate change, we can contribute to the global efforts to address this pressing issue and ensure a sustainable and prosperous planet for future generations.

B. Emphasizing the Role of Human Activity in Accelerating Climate Change
In the narrative that the climate is not changing in an unprecedented and catastrophic manner, it is crucial to highlight the significant role of human activity in accelerating climate change. While natural climate variations have occurred throughout Earth's history, the current changes are largely driven by human-induced factors, leading to profound consequences for our planet.

Greenhouse Gas Emissions: Human Contribution to Climate Change
Human activities, particularly the burning of fossil fuels such as coal, oil, and natural gas, have released vast amounts of greenhouse gases into the atmosphere. Carbon dioxide (CO_2) is the primary greenhouse gas responsible for trapping heat in the Earth's atmosphere. Since the Industrial Revolution, CO_2 concentrations have increased by more than 40%, reaching levels unseen in hundreds of thousands of years. Other greenhouse gases, such as methane (CH_4) and nitrous oxide (N_2O), also contribute to the enhanced greenhouse effect.

Anthropogenic Forcing: Amplifying Climate Changes
The influence of human activities on climate extends beyond greenhouse gas emissions. Land-use changes, such as deforestation and urbanization, alter the surface properties of the Earth, leading to changes in energy balance and atmospheric circulation patterns. Industrial processes, including the production of cement and chemicals, emit additional greenhouse gases and aerosols that can further impact the climate system.

Positive Feedback Mechanisms: Amplifying Climate Sensitivity
Human-induced climate change can trigger positive feedback mechanisms, amplifying the warming effect. For example, as temperatures rise, melting ice caps and glaciers reduce the Earth's albedo, causing more sunlight to be absorbed and leading to further warming. This positive feedback loop contributes to accelerated ice melt, sea-level rise, and altered climate patterns.

Impacts on Temperature and Precipitation: Evidence of Human Influence
Scientific research and climate models provide robust evidence of the human influence on temperature and precipitation patterns. Studies have shown that the observed increase in global average temperature is primarily due to human activities. Extreme weather events, such as heatwaves, droughts, and heavy rainfall, have also been linked to climate change.

Ocean Acidification: Human Impact on Marine Ecosystems
Human-induced carbon dioxide emissions not only contribute to global warming but also lead to ocean acidification. As the oceans absorb CO_2 from the atmosphere, the pH of seawater decreases, affecting marine life, particularly organisms that build shells or skeletons from calcium carbonate. Coral reefs, which provide habitat for a vast array of marine species, are particularly vulnerable to ocean acidification.

Sea-Level Rise: Human Contribution to Coastal Vulnerability
Human-induced climate change has contributed to rising sea levels, primarily through the thermal expansion of seawater and the melting of ice caps and glaciers. Global mean sea level has been rising at an accelerated rate over the past century, posing significant threats to coastal regions, including increased coastal erosion, inundation, and saltwater intrusion into freshwater resources.

In summary, the narrative of the climate not changing in an unprecedented and catastrophic manner aligns with the scientific understanding of human activities as a significant driver of climate change. The burning of fossil fuels, land-use changes, and industrial processes have contributed to increased greenhouse gas concentrations, amplifying the greenhouse effect and leading to a range of impacts on temperature, precipitation, ocean acidity, and sea-level rise. By acknowledging the role of human activity, we can better comprehend the urgency for global action and the need to transition to sustainable practices that mitigate climate change and safeguard the future of our planet.

C. Urgency for Global Action and Sustainable Practices

Amidst the narrative that the climate is not changing in an unprecedented and catastrophic manner, it is crucial to recognize the urgency for global action and the adoption of sustainable practices. The scientific evidence overwhelmingly supports the need for immediate and concerted efforts to address climate change and its far-reaching impacts on the environment, societies, and economies.

Projected Future Scenarios: Heightening Concerns
Climate models and projections provide valuable insights into potential future scenarios based on different emission trajectories. These scenarios highlight the magnitude of the challenges we face if we continue with business-as-usual practices. They indicate a range of adverse effects, including more frequent and intense heatwaves, extreme weather events, water scarcity, loss of biodiversity, and disruptions to agricultural systems. Understanding these projected outcomes emphasizes the importance of proactive measures to mitigate and adapt to climate change.

Mitigation Strategies: Reducing Greenhouse Gas Emissions
Mitigation strategies aim to reduce greenhouse gas emissions and limit the extent of climate change. They involve transitioning to low-carbon energy sources, improving energy efficiency, promoting sustainable transportation, and adopting practices that minimize emissions from industries, agriculture, and waste management. The Intergovernmental Panel on Climate Change (IPCC) estimates that to limit global warming to well below 2 degrees Celsius, we must achieve substantial emissions reductions, aiming for carbon neutrality by mid-century.

Renewable Energy Transition: A Pathway to Sustainability
The transition to renewable energy sources plays a pivotal role in mitigating climate change. Solar, wind, hydro, geothermal, and biomass energy offer sustainable alternatives to fossil fuels. By scaling up renewable energy infrastructure and enhancing research and development in clean technologies, we can significantly reduce greenhouse gas emissions and decrease our reliance on non-renewable resources.

Sustainable Land and Forest Management: Preserving Ecosystems
Preserving and sustainably managing our land and forests are essential for climate change mitigation and adaptation. Forests act as carbon sinks, absorbing CO_2 from the atmosphere and storing it in vegetation and soils. Reducing deforestation rates, implementing reforestation and afforestation programs, and promoting sustainable land management practices help maintain ecosystem health, conserve biodiversity, and enhance carbon sequestration.

Climate Finance: Mobilizing Resources for Action
Addressing climate change requires substantial financial resources to support mitigation and adaptation efforts, especially in developing countries. Climate finance mechanisms, such as the Green Climate Fund and international cooperation initiatives, aim to mobilize financial resources for climate-related projects and support vulnerable communities in adapting to climate impacts. Investing in climate-friendly technologies, infrastructure, and resilience-building measures is crucial for achieving sustainable development goals.

Ethics, Justice, and Equity: Ensuring Fairness in Climate Action
Climate change disproportionately affects vulnerable populations, exacerbating social and economic inequalities. Addressing climate change must go hand in hand with considerations of ethics, justice, and equity. It is crucial to ensure that climate policies and actions prioritize the needs of the most affected communities, support their adaptation efforts, and foster inclusive and participatory decision-making processes.

In conclusion, the narrative of the climate not changing in an unprecedented and catastrophic manner should not overshadow the urgent need for global action. The scientific evidence highlights the impacts of human activities on the climate system and the projected risks associated with unchecked climate change. Mitigation strategies, renewable energy transition, sustainable land management, climate finance, and considerations of ethics and equity are all integral to addressing climate change effectively. By embracing sustainable practices, fostering international collaboration, and advocating for climate action, we can strive towards a sustainable and resilient future for current and future generations.

D. Encouragement for Readers to Become Climate Change Advocates

As we come to the end of this comprehensive exploration of climate change, it is essential to empower individuals to become climate change advocates in their own right. Each one of us has a role to play in raising awareness, driving change, and promoting sustainable practices within our communities and beyond. Here are some key considerations and actions that can make a difference:

1. Education and Awareness: Knowledge is a powerful tool for change. Educate yourself about climate change, its causes, impacts, and solutions. Stay updated with the latest scientific research and policy developments. Engage in discussions, share reliable information, and raise awareness among your family, friends, and social networks.

2. Sustainable Lifestyle Choices: Evaluate your own carbon footprint and strive to make sustainable lifestyle choices. Reduce energy consumption by using energy-efficient appliances, practicing smart heating and cooling habits, and opting for renewable energy sources whenever possible. Minimize waste generation, recycle, and support circular economy principles. Choose sustainable transportation options, such as walking, cycling, or using public transportation, and consider reducing meat consumption to lower your dietary carbon footprint.

3. Active Citizenship: Engage with local and national policymakers to advocate for strong climate policies. Join or support organizations working towards climate action. Attend community meetings, participate in public consultations, and express your concerns about the environment. Vote for leaders who prioritize climate change as a critical issue and support sustainable policies.

4. Support Renewable Energy: Invest in renewable energy sources for your home or consider community solar initiatives. Encourage your workplace, school, or local institutions to transition to clean energy sources. By supporting the growth of renewable energy infrastructure, you contribute to reducing greenhouse gas emissions and accelerating the shift towards a low-carbon future.

5. Promote Climate Resilience: Help build resilience in your community to adapt to climate change impacts. Support initiatives that focus on climate-smart agriculture, water conservation, disaster preparedness, and sustainable urban planning. Encourage green spaces, tree planting, and the preservation of natural habitats to enhance biodiversity and mitigate climate risks.

6. Engage with Indigenous Knowledge: Recognize and respect the traditional ecological wisdom held by indigenous communities. Collaborate with indigenous peoples in the development and implementation of climate solutions, respecting their rights and knowledge systems. Indigenous communities have long-standing relationships with the land and possess valuable insights into sustainable resource management.

7. Consumer Choices: Make conscious choices as a consumer. Support companies that prioritize sustainability and ethical practices. Consider the environmental impact of the products you purchase, and opt for eco-friendly alternatives. Support local and sustainable agriculture, fair trade, and responsible manufacturing practices.

8. Inspire Others: Lead by example and inspire others to take action. Share success stories of climate initiatives, highlight the benefits of sustainable practices, and encourage others to join the movement. Engage in conversations, organize awareness events, and leverage social media platforms to amplify the message of climate action.

By becoming climate change advocates, we can contribute to a collective effort that transcends borders, cultures, and generations. Our individual actions, when combined, have the power to create meaningful change. Let us embrace the narrative that the climate is not changing in an unprecedented and catastrophic manner, while recognizing the urgent need for action and working together towards a sustainable and resilient future.

Appendices

A: Glossary of Key Terms

To enhance the understanding of climate change and its related concepts, the following glossary provides definitions for key terms used throughout this document ;

1. Climate Change: Refers to long-term changes in temperature, precipitation patterns, wind patterns, and other aspects of the Earth's climate system, primarily caused by human activities such as the burning of fossil fuels and deforestation.

2. Greenhouse Effect: The process by which certain gases in the Earth's atmosphere trap heat from the sun, leading to a warming effect. This natural phenomenon is essential for maintaining the Earth's temperature within a habitable range, but human activities have intensified the greenhouse effect, leading to accelerated warming.

3. Global Warming: The long-term increase in Earth's average surface temperature due to human-induced greenhouse gas emissions. It is a consequence of the enhanced greenhouse effect.

4. Carbon Dioxide (CO_2): The primary greenhouse gas released by human activities, particularly the burning of fossil fuels. CO_2 is a significant contributor to global warming and climate change.

5. Greenhouse Gases (GHGs): Gases that trap heat in the atmosphere and contribute to the greenhouse effect. Besides carbon dioxide, other important greenhouse gases include methane (CH_4), nitrous oxide (N_2O), and fluorinated gases.

6. Paris Agreement: An international treaty signed in 2015, aiming to limit global warming well below 2 degrees Celsius above pre-industrial levels and pursue efforts to limit the temperature increase to 1.5 degrees Celsius. It emphasizes global cooperation in reducing greenhouse gas emissions and adapting to the impacts of climate change.

7. Mitigation: Actions taken to reduce or prevent greenhouse gas emissions and limit the extent of climate change. Examples include transitioning to renewable energy sources, improving energy efficiency, and adopting sustainable land management practices.

8. Adaptation: Strategies and measures taken to adjust and respond to the impacts of climate change. Adaptation focuses on building resilience and reducing vulnerability in various sectors such as agriculture, water resources, and infrastructure.

9. IPCC: The Intergovernmental Panel on Climate Change is a scientific body established by the United Nations and the World Meteorological Organization. It assesses the scientific, technical, and socioeconomic aspects of climate change and provides policymakers with objective information to inform climate action.

10. Climate Models: Computer simulations that represent the Earth's climate system and its various components. Climate models are used to understand

past climate patterns, project future climate scenarios, and assess the impacts of different factors on the climate system.

11. Carbon Footprint: The total amount of greenhouse gases, especially carbon dioxide, emitted directly or indirectly by an individual, organization, product, or activity. It is measured in carbon dioxide equivalent (CO_2e) and is used to assess the impact of human activities on climate change.

12. Renewable Energy: Energy derived from natural sources that are constantly replenished, such as sunlight, wind, water, and geothermal heat. Renewable energy is considered environmentally friendly because it produces fewer greenhouse gas emissions compared to fossil fuels.

This glossary provides a foundation for understanding the key terms and concepts related to climate change. It is important to familiarize oneself with these terms to engage in meaningful discussions and further explore the topic.

Please note that this glossary is not exhaustive and may not cover all terms used in the field of climate science. Further reading and research are recommended for a comprehensive understanding of climate change and its related terminology.

B. Additional Resources for Further Reading

For readers who wish to explore climate change in more depth and broaden their knowledge on the subject, the following list provides a selection of recommended resources, including books, scientific reports, websites, and documentaries:

1. Books:
   - "The Uninhabitable Earth: Life After Warming" by David Wallace-Wells
   - "This Changes Everything: Capitalism vs. The Climate" by Naomi Klein
   - "The Sixth Extinction: An Unnatural History" by Elizabeth Kolbert
   - "Drawdown: The Most Comprehensive Plan Ever Proposed to Reverse Global Warming" edited by Paul Hawken
   - "The Weather Makers: How Man Is Changing the Climate and What It Means for Life on Earth" by Tim Flannery

2. Scientific Reports and Assessments:
   - Intergovernmental Panel on Climate Change (IPCC) Assessment Reports: These comprehensive reports provide an overview of the current state of scientific knowledge on climate change, its impacts, and potential mitigation and adaptation strategies. They are available on the IPCC website.

3. Websites:
   - NASA Climate Change: The NASA Climate Change website offers a wealth of information on climate science, including research, data visualizations, and educational resources.
   - NOAA Climate.gov: The NOAA Climate.gov website provides climate news, data, and educational materials to help understand climate variability and change.
   - United Nations Framework Convention on Climate Change (UNFCCC): The UNFCCC website provides updates on international climate negotiations, policies, and actions.

4. Documentaries:
   - "An Inconvenient Truth" (2006): A documentary featuring former Vice President Al Gore, highlighting the urgency and impacts of climate change.

- "Chasing Ice" (2012): The film follows environmental photographer James Balog as he documents the melting glaciers around the world.
- "Before the Flood" (2016): Produced by National Geographic, this documentary explores the impacts of climate change and potential solutions.
- "Our Planet" (2019): A Netflix series narrated by David Attenborough, showcasing the beauty of Earth's diverse ecosystems and addressing the challenges they face due to climate change.

These resources offer valuable insights into the science, impacts, and solutions related to climate change. They present diverse perspectives and allow readers to delve deeper into specific topics of interest. It is recommended to critically evaluate the information and cross-reference with reputable scientific sources for a comprehensive understanding of climate change.

C. Data and Charts Supporting Key Concepts

In order to provide readers with access to data and visual representations of key concepts discussed throughout this guide, the following section presents a selection of data sets and charts:

1. Global Temperature Anomalies:
   - Data Source: NASA Goddard Institute for Space Studies (GISS)
   - Chart: A line graph illustrating the year-by-year changes in global surface temperature anomalies relative to the 20th-century average.

2. Atmospheric Carbon Dioxide (CO2) Concentration:
   - Data Source: Mauna Loa Observatory, Scripps Institution of Oceanography
   - Chart: A time series graph showing the continuous increase in atmospheric CO2 concentration measured at the Mauna Loa Observatory.

3. Sea Level Rise:
   - Data Source: National Oceanic and Atmospheric Administration (NOAA)
   - Chart: A bar chart demonstrating the average global sea level rise over the past century, based on long-term tide gauge measurements and satellite observations.

4. Extreme Weather Events:
   - Data Source: Munich Re Group, United Nations Office for Disaster Risk Reduction (UNDRR)

- Chart: A stacked column chart displaying the number and economic losses of extreme weather events (e.g., hurricanes, floods, heatwaves) over a specified period.

5. Glacier Retreat:
   - Data Source: World Glacier Monitoring Service (WGMS)
   - Chart: A series of maps or satellite images showcasing the retreat of selected glaciers around the world over the past few decades.

6. Renewable Energy Capacity:
   - Data Source: International Renewable Energy Agency (IREA)
   - Chart: A bar or pie chart representing the global installed capacity of renewable energy sources (solar, wind, hydro, etc.) and their contribution to the overall energy mix.

These data sets and charts offer visual evidence and scientific measurements supporting the understanding of various climate change phenomena and their impacts. The inclusion of empirical data enhances the credibility and accuracy of the information presented in this guide. Readers are encouraged to explore these data sources further for more comprehensive analyses and insights.

D. Acknowledgments
Writing a comprehensive guide on climate change and its impacts requires the collaboration and support of various individuals and organizations. We would like to

express our gratitude to the following people and institutions for their contributions to this guide:

1. Scientific Experts: We extend our appreciation to the numerous scientists and researchers who have dedicated their careers to studying climate change. Their valuable insights, research findings, and peer-reviewed studies have served as the foundation for the scientific understanding of climate change and its impacts.

2. Data Providers: We would like to acknowledge the organizations and institutions that collect, curate, and share climate-related data. Their efforts in monitoring temperature records, greenhouse gas concentrations, sea levels, and other key variables enable us to analyze and assess the state of the climate system.

3. International and National Institutions: We are grateful for the work of international organizations such as the Intergovernmental Panel on Climate Change (IPCC), the United Nations Framework Convention on Climate Change (UNFCCC), and national bodies responsible for climate research and policy development. Their efforts in synthesizing scientific knowledge, facilitating international cooperation, and promoting climate action are instrumental in addressing the challenges of climate change.

4. Indigenous Communities and Local Knowledge Holders: We acknowledge the traditional ecological wisdom and knowledge of indigenous communities

around the world. Their deep connection to the land and their understanding of ecosystem dynamics contribute to our broader understanding of sustainable practices and resilience-building in the face of climate change.

5. Reviewers and Feedback Contributors: We would like to thank the individuals who provided valuable feedback and suggestions during the review process of this guide. Their input has helped shape and improve the content, ensuring its accuracy and clarity.

6. Editorial and Design Team: Our sincere appreciation goes to the editorial and design team involved in the creation of this guide. Their expertise, attention to detail, and commitment to quality have contributed to the overall presentation and accessibility of the information.

Lastly, we extend our gratitude to all readers who have engaged with this guide. We hope that the knowledge and insights gained from this resource empower you to better understand the complexities of climate change and inspire you to take meaningful action in addressing this global challenge.

Together, through collaboration, awareness, and action, we can strive for a sustainable and resilient future for our planet and future generations.